Golden Wind

GOLDEN WIND

Zen Talks

by Eido Shimano Roshi

edited by Janis Levine

JAPAN PUBLICATIONS, INC.

© 1979 in Japan by The Zen Studies Society, Inc.

Published by
JAPAN PUBLICATIONS, INC., Tokyo, Japan

Distributors:
UNITED STATES: *Kodansha International/USA, Ltd., through Harper & Row, Publishers, Inc., 10 East 53rd Street, New York, New York 10022.* SOUTH AMERICA: *Harper & Row, Publishers, Inc., International Department.* CANADA: *Fitzhenry & Whiteside Ltd., 150 Lesmill Road, Don Mills, Ontario M3B 2T6.* MEXICO AND CENTRAL AMERICA: *HARLA S. A. de C. V., Apartado 30-546, Mexico 4, D. F.* BRITISH ISLES: *International Book Distributors Ltd., 66 Wood Lane End, Hemel Hempstead, Herts HPZ 4RG.* EUROPEAN CONTINENT: *Boxerbooks, Inc., Limmatstrasse 111, 8031 Zurich.* AUSTRALIA AND NEW ZEALAND: *Book Wise (Australia) Pty. Ltd., 104-8 Sussex Street, Sydney 2000.* THE FAR EAST AND JAPAN: *Japan Publications Trading Co., Ltd., 1-2-1, Sarugaku-cho, Chiyoda-ku, Tokyo 101.*

First Printing: September 1979

ISBN 0-87040-449-0

Printed in U.S.A.

To New York Zendo Shobo-ji on the occasion of its tenth anniversary, September 15, 1978, this book is respectfully dedicated.

Let True Dharma Continue,
Universal Sangha Relation
International Dai Bosatsu Zendo
Become Complete.

Contents

Introduction

This is a book of *teishos*. Brusquely rendered into English, a teisho is a Zen lecture. Those who are familiar with the culture of the Orient, especially Japan, will better understand the nature of teisho when I say that teisho is as much just a "lecture" as a tea ceremony is just a "ceremony," aikido is just a "martial art" and a Noh drama is just a "play." However, I must assume that many, if not most of you have had little or no direct contact with Japanese culture or traditional Zen practice. Therefore in order to prepare you for the pages to follow, it is my task here to present a word portrait of the teisho—a portrait that will, I hope, enable you to create within yourselves the proper attitude needed to reap the maximum benefits from a book of this kind.

The word teisho is composed of two Chinese ideographs. The first, *tei*, means "to carry" and the second, *sho*, means "to preach," "to recite," or "to declare." Putting the meaning of the two ideographs together, we can arrive at the primary function of a teisho—to carry and preach the true teachings of the Buddha. Eido Shimano Roshi suggested this translation: "to carry and declare the point." What point? Read or listen to a teisho yourself and, at least intellectually, you will come to the point of the matter of Zen, in other words, you will find nothing less than the very essence of Mind.

The "sho" ideograph of teisho immediately conveys the communication aspect—the lecture or mouth to ear communication. What makes teisho so unique is the "tei." Why "carry"? What is carried and who carries it? When most people encounter Zen for the first time, they are usually struck by certain elusive qualities of both its teachers and its texts. Nothing seems to be explained in a logical manner. "XYZ" no longer equals "XYZ." "Yes" is "No" and "No" is "Yes." There is no place to anchor a conceptual understanding. There is just no convenient statement informing us that Zen is this or that. Like no other religion, thought or philosophy, Zen is simply not concerned with intellectual understanding. The point of Zen can only be learned through personal experience—an experience usually attained through years and years of a specialized meditation practice known as *zazen*. Zazen is the heartbeat of Zen and experience is its flesh and blood.

A Zen experience opens our minds to another viewpoint of reality. It awakens us to the Truth of reality, the Truth of who we really are, the Truth of life and death, the Truth of the nature of the universe and all things residing therein. Like any other experience, the Zen experience, with continual zazen, happens again and again. Each time, the understanding becomes more clear, becomes more a part of the life and person of the experiencer. Eventually, it becomes apparent in his every thought, deed, and word, through every moment of his life, day and night. Every thought, deed, and word "carries" True understanding.

In the strictest sense of the word, a teisho may only be carried and delivered by a Zen master, a *roshi*. In the Rinzai school of Zen Buddhism, a student of Zen receives the title "roshi" only when his teacher considers him sufficiently experienced. The Truth has become so permeated throughout his total being that it has virtually become the substance, the flesh and blood of the Zen student. He is a roshi, a Zen master, a master of the True understanding. The teisho of such a man not only "declares" the point with language, but most importantly, the man "carries" the point with his body, heart, and mind.

When they appear on the printed page, the words of a teisho are the apparent vehicle of communication. However, like the script of a play, the combination of a skillful director, a sensitive actor, and a receptive audience is required to breathe into the words a living moment of dimensional reality. The roshi is, so to speak, the director, actor, and playwright of a teisho. The *sangha*, his students, are the audience and the *sesshin*, an intensive zazen retreat, is the stage. The total aliveness of a teisho simply cannot be fully conveyed on a piece of paper.

As Eido Roshi, as he is known by his students, delivers his teisho, a look, a change in intonation, a pause, a gesture, a clap of his hands, a sip from his cup of tea all serve to enhance the power of his talk. An unexpected song from a nearby bird, a sudden gust of wind shaking the trees and windows, rain pattering on the roof, snow whitening the world, the blare of car horns in New York City traffic, the subtle fragrance of burning incense—each of these, a teisho unto itself, adds a special fullness to the mood, a special flavor to the Roshi's talk. An editor's pen cannot capture such scenery. The world of the written word is limited to a sheet of paper, whereas the real world, the world in which the original teisho took place, is both unpredictable and limitless. The teisho reflects the limitlessness.

Perhaps now you can understand when I confess to you that what you are about to read is only one surface of a teisho. Unfortunately, you will miss the depth of the moment that caught the words and made them live. You must provide your own moment of life as you read. That original moment can never be recreated in print, for it was born of Eido Roshi's physical and spiritual presence and it was nurtured by the very special quiet of the room in which he spoke.

Teishos are always given during sesshins, for good cause. Eido Roshi delivered the teishos recorded on the pages of this book during either seven-day or weekend sesshins held at Dai Bosatsu Zendo in the Catskill Mountains of New York State and at the New York Zendo in New York City. From early morning, usually 4 A.M., till evening, usually 9 P.M., sesshin attendants follow a precise schedule of zazen, chanting, eating and *dokusan* (private consultation with a roshi). The teisho is given once every day. The students do not speak, do not look around and do not participate in any other distracting pursuits. It is a time of intense, inward concentration.

The bulk of the day and evening during a sesshin is devoted to zazen. Even while the teisho is being given, the students continue to sit in zazen. Although there may be fifty or sixty people in one room, the quiet is pronounced. The teisho, almost miraculously, does not interrupt this quiet. Rather, it adds to the intensity of silence. Each person's zazen also contributes to this indescribable atmosphere.

As the days progress and as each person's zazen becomes deeper and purer, the atmosphere of sesshin takes on unbelievable proportions—so sharp, so clear, so alive, so calm. And although the words of the teisho are coming from the Roshi's mouth, the feeling of his words seems to emanate from all who are actively listening. The teisho creates a mood and the mood creates a teisho. In the final analysis, it is zazen which creates both.

Again, I must emphasize this crucial point: I am not recreating the scene of a teisho simply as a writing exercise. My purpose is to give you a glimpse of the forces which work towards determining the many facets of a teisho so that you may read this book with the right kind of perspective. If you do not practice zazen, it is a good idea to calm yourself by concentrating for a while on your own breath and to sit with a straight back before starting to read. Eido Roshi himself suggests that you read this book as slowly as possible. Even one teisho a day is enough.

Although the teishos certainly contain interesting background information to the koans and although they also serve to clarify much of the mystique associated with the style and language of Zen lore, the teishos, most importantly, contain information that your body and mind will soak up without your even being aware of it until, perhaps, some later time—when you are ready. As you read, chew each teisho slowly. Appreciate its flavor.

Another special quality about Eido Roshi's teishos is that throughout, he provides sound, practical advice on how to proceed with zazen practice so that the student of Zen may gain a stronger hold on his own life, as well as a compassionate understanding of the nature of all the creatures and things of this vast universe. Eido Roshi teaches us how to perfect those qualities necessary to strengthen our ability to live as human beings in a world of unexpected twists and turns.

All but one of the teishos included in this book are based upon koans chosen from three traditional Chinese Zen texts, *Rinzai Roku* or *The Recorded Sayings of Master Rinzai, Hekigan Roku* or *The Blue Rock Collection,* and *Mumonkan* or *The Gateless Gate.* Each chapter, or case, of the two latter texts consists of a koan, usually in the form of a dialogue, and commentaries composed by the compilers. These commentaries appear in both prose and verse. The *Rinzai Roku* consists of five parts: The Preface, Discourses, Sermons, Dialogues, and Pilgrimages. Although Eido Roshi uses the koans as a general theme for his teishos and supplies his own commentaries based on his intuitive understanding of Zen, he declares and carries the "point" in his introductory statements. Pay close attention to these remarks, for these are the teisho. Only when the original verse and comment supplies extra emphasis to his own words without being overtly redundant, or when they add a unique point of interest relevant to the teisho, does Eido Roshi include them. This book should therefore not be viewed as an interpretive analysis of the several Zen texts. To exclude or include whatever he wishes in order to clarify the point is the license given a Zen master. Such prerogative is not necessarily open to a professor of Zen Buddhism, for his basic goal is to expound and explain.

The order of the teishos as they appear in the book is not based upon their original order as they appeared in the Zen texts. Neither are they arranged chronologically. Eido Roshi, again using his special license, arranged them in an order best suited for book form. The first few are in a sense introductory, the last few, climactic. The order, therefore, being neither random nor contrived, best suits the point. In various ways, it carries and declares it.

Eido Shimano Roshi is a Japanese Rinzai Zen monk who has been living and teaching in the United States for nearly two decades. English is his second language—a cause for both praise and blame, as you like. In my capacity as editor, my job was not so much to produce a book of perfect English syntax. Rather it was to transcribe Eido Roshi's spoken word for the printed page, without sacrificing his approach to the English language and without impeding his own style of teaching —witty, direct and down to earth. His words, when he speaks them, ignite within his students the fire of zazen practice.

Working very closely with Eido Roshi, I have tried to eliminate most of the awkwardness of Japanese-English while overlooking some other linguistic deviations. Hopefully, the outcome of my work, whether good or bad English, is Eido Roshi on the printed page, much the same as he appears to his students during a teisho. You will notice that his grasp of English leaves him enough room to invent his own idioms appropriate for certain ideas inherent in Zen. He invented these idioms in order to convey the Zen point of view in the most concise and direct fashion. Here are a few: "the readiness of time," "the plain factuality," "THIS matter," and "as-it-is-ness." The meaning of these phrases and others becomes clear enough when read in the proper context.

Included in the appendix are two pieces by the well-known eighteenth-century Japanese Zen master, Hakuin Ekaku Zenji. When

Hakuin began his practice of Zen, he discovered that Zen Buddhism, as it existed in the famous temples of Japan, had been reduced to an intellectual and artistic exercise. As a path to True understanding, it was virtually dead. Hakuin proceeded to reestablish and reorganize the traditional way of koan study. He emphasized the importance of regular zazen practice. Without zazen, Zen is just an empty shell of puzzling but beautiful words. With it, Zen brings a profound peace of mind to all who endure its strenuous practice.

The *Rohatsu Exhortation* is a series of extemporaneous talks given by Master Hakuin during a Rohatsu Sesshin. To my knowledge, this is the first time that the *Rohatsu Exhortation* has appeared in English translation. Rohatsu means "the eighth of December," the day that Buddha Shakyamuni had his great enlightenment. Traditionally, every Zen monastery holds an annual Rohatsu Sesshin to commemorate and to recreate the Buddha's enlightenment. Held during the coldest season of the year, it is the most vigorous sesshin of all—less sleep and rest, more and more zazen.

Usually, once or twice a day during a sesshin, the roshi gives a short impromptu talk to his students while they are sitting in the zendo. These talks act as powerful inducements to continue the struggle for supremacy over ego. The *Rohatsu Exhortation* is a compilation of this kind of spontaneous encouragement. Every year during our own Rohatsu Sesshin, before the long evening of zazen begins, Eido Roshi reads one chapter of this work each night. I can only say that its power to inspire is remarkable.

Hakuin's *Song of Zazen*, the second work included in the appendix, clearly speaks for itself. To begin the teisho, all sesshin attendants participate in a relatively brief service of *sutra* chanting. The effect of the harmonious combination of everyone's voice serves to complement the cohesiveness of the atmosphere. At Dai Bosatsu Zendo and New York Zendo, the very last piece that we recite before Eido Roshi begins his talk is this *Song of Zazen*. Since it is nothing less than Hakuin's personal introduction to any and all teishos, its inclusion in a book of teishos must certainly be considered appropriate.

At this point I must express my special gratitude to Eido Roshi. Maintaining two zendos, conducting six or seven week-long sesshins and at least that many weekend sesshins in one year, and performing various other works that a spiritual leader necessarily finds himself involved with, Eido Roshi is an extremely hard working and busy person. Initially, he was not to be involved in the preparation of this book. He was to serve in an advisory capacity in order that extra work not be imposed upon him. However, as I began the editing I found that his active participation was necessary. So it happened that he had to spend at least as much time on this book as I did, thus adding more burdens to his already full schedule. Even so, his enthusiasm and spirit were great. Now I can honestly say that this is Eido Roshi's book, this is his Zen talk. Even the koans, comments, and verses from the Chinese Zen texts are his translations.

Finally, to prepare this book from talk to tape to typewriter also required the assistance of many wonderful Dharma brothers and sisters. I would like to express my special thanks to Myoan Lillian Friedman who transcribed most of the teishos, and to Chigetsu Ruth Lilienthal who helped her decipher some faulty recordings. Also thanks to Eshin Brenda Lukeman, Jinen Nancy Merck and Bill and Dorothy Grossman for their transcription work, and to Daishin Stephen Levine for his assistance in proofreading the final manuscript.

Soshin Janis Levine
New York Zendo Shobo-ji
February 1, 1978

Selected Teishos
of
Eido Shimano Roshi

Ummon's Golden Wind

The Blue Rock Collection: Case 27

The Koan:
A monk asked Ummon, "What will happen when the leaves fall
and the trees become bare?"
Ummon said, "Golden Wind!"

The Teisho:
As for zazen practice in the Mahayana,
We have no words to praise it fully . . . .

Even those who have practiced it for just one sitting
Will see all their evil karma erased . . . .

How boundless the cleared sky of samadhi!
How transparent the perfect moonlight of the Fourfold Wisdom!

By the sixth day of sesshin these words from Hakuin Zenji's *Song of Zazen* sound more and more true. Many superficial thoughts have, by now, gone. We know that when the clouds open up for one minute, we have one minute of sunshine. Two minutes of a cloudless sky gives us two minutes of sunshine. In the same way, even one minute of zazen makes a one-minute Buddha, one minute of the light of wisdom.

Today we are introduced to Ummon Bun'en Zenji (862/4–949). Among the many outstanding Zen masters in China, this Ummon Bun'en Zenji expresses Zen in the most elegant, refined, poetic and, above all, attractive manner. As some of you may be unfamiliar with Ummon, let me begin the introductions by means of a story.

According to the custom of the times, as a young monk Ummon traveled around the countryside of China, visiting one master after another, searching for a congenial teacher. Congeniality between teacher and student is very important. One day, he came to a small hut where Master Bokushu was living the life of a hermit, practicing all by himself. Although the hermit's life does seem to be an excuse for avoiding responsibilities, in the case of Bokushu, he was actually waiting. He was waiting for the appropriate student to come so that he could give him proper guidance in order that the Dharma might continue to flourish. Each teacher has different karma and different capacities. A one-gallon container has not the capacity to hold ten gallons of water. This Bokushu surely knew his own capacity and his own way.

At any rate, one day the traveling monk, Ummon, approached Bokushu's hut. In those days, if someone wanted to study with a teacher, there were no application forms to fill out and mail in. Everything was spontaneous. Inside the hut, Bokushu was sitting, waiting, ready to give immediate dokusan if anyone were to come. Ummon knocked.

"Who is it?"

"My name is Bun'en." At that time, Ummon was called only by the name Bun'en.

"Come in."

As soon as Bun'en entered the room, Bokushu stood up, grabbed him and said, "Speak! Speak!"

Not only was Bun'en surprised, but in fact, he did not know what to say. Seeing this young man's reaction, Bokushu immediately pushed him out and slammed shut the sliding doors. This is how real dokusan should be conducted. Nowadays everything is so well organized. Organization makes things run smoothly but, at the same time, takes away something from the vital spirit of spontaneity. Everyone knows that when they come to dokusan they will not be grabbed and bodily thrown out. So everyone, after a few dokusan experiences, comes with a certain amount of self-assuredness, knowing what to expect.

Some days passed, during which time Ummon Bun'en was most likely sitting somewhere near the cottage, thinking, "What does that mean, 'SPEAK!'?"

If I were to say to you, "Speak!" you would reply, "Speak? Speak about what?" Ummon did not think like this. Just SPEAK! SPEAK!

Ummon sat and sat and finally decided to pay a second visit. Again he knocked.

"Who is it?"

"Bun'en."

"Come in."

And once more Bokushu shouted, "Speak!" as soon as Ummon entered. And once more Ummon could not speak and once more Bokushu pushed him out and slammed shut the sliding doors.

A few more days passed—exactly how many days passed, no one knows. For the third time Ummon decided to try again, but this time his zazen had become more intense, more calm, and more lucid.

The same dialogue ensued, but this time when Bokushu threw Bun'en out and shut the door, the young monk's right leg was still inside the hut. Bun'en screamed, "OUCH!" It is at this very instant that he understood. Thus Ummon Bun'en Zenji, as we know him, was born.

In those days there were no organized seven-day sesshins, neither were there organized dokusans held three times a day. Only a monk who was truly ready would come to see the master. Dokusan, to describe it briefly, is a short period of consultation or confrontation with a Zen master. Nowadays everything has to be defined. Definitions do make things clearer but they also establish limits. Real dokusan is far more than either consultation or confrontation. Someone came to dokusan and said, "I have nothing for consultation. I have nothing for confrontation. I even have nothing to say." Of course, I too had nothing to say, but in this non-saying we spoke more than could possibly be said in even one hour of talk, talk, talk. Even better than this, someone showed up and, putting his palms together, chanted the *Great Vows for All:*

> *Shu jo mu hen sei gan do*
> *Bo no mu jin sei gan dan*
> *Ho mon mu ryo sei gan gaku*
> *Butsu do mu jo sei gan jo.*

And then that person said, "That's all."

Indeed, THAT'S ALL!

We come here for various reasons. Some of us are seeking self-realization. That's fine. Some of us are after spiritual growth. Not bad. Some may be longing for seven days of silence. Okay. We often speak about the objectives of our zazen practice. But again, if we define, if we spell out, we bind the free activity of the Zen spirit. Yet if we don't spell it out, the direction is unclear. This is always a dilemma. If we were to spell out the objectives of our practice, they would be the *Great Vows for All:*

> *However innumerable all beings are,*
>   *I vow to save them all;*
> *However inexhaustible my delusions are,*
>   *I vow to extinguish them all;*
> *However immeasurable the Dharma Teachings are,*
>   *I vow to master them all;*
> *However endless the Buddha's Way is,*
>   *I vow to follow it.*

THAT'S ALL!

Some of you may say. "How can I save the others before I am saved myself?" You can save electricity before you become enlightened; you can save a drop of water before you attain self-realization; you can actually save so many, many things prior to your spiritual growth. I don't know if Bokushu would have accepted "Shu jo mu hen sei gan do" as a reply to his "SPEAK!" but if not this, then what!

Later, this Bun'en, the traveling monk, came to live on Ummon Mountain and so people called him Ummon Bun'en Zenji.

In the beginning of this teisho, I called Ummon the master of the elegant, refined, poetic, and attractive Zen expression. I may add other adjectives like direct, simple, and profound to describe him, but no matter how many I might use, I am still left frustrated. There are no words to sufficiently describe this great master's talent. Let me give you a few examples of his dialogues so that you can judge for yourself.

> *A monk asked Ummon, "What is the kind of talk that transcends Buddhas and Patriarchs?"*
> *Ummon replied, "Rice cake!"*

A monk asked Ummon, "What is Ummon's melody?"
Ummon replied, "The twenty-fifth of December!"

A monk asked Ummon, "What is the samadhi of each individual thing?"
Ummon replied, "Rice in bowl, water in pail!"

A monk asked Ummon, "What is Buddha?"
Ummon replied, "Toilet paper!"

A monk asked Ummon, "No thoughts have risen. Are there any faults or not?"
Ummon said, "Mount Sumeru!"

Ummon said to his disciples, "I do not ask you to say anything about before the fifteenth day of the month, but say something about after the fifteenth day of the month."
Because no monk could reply, Ummon answered himself and said, "Every day is a good day!"

On another occasion Ummon said, "However wonderful a thing is, it may be that it is better not to have it at all."

And today's koan:
A monk asked Ummon, "What will happen when the leaves fall and the trees become bare?"
Ummon said, "Golden Wind!"

This koan may be relatively easy to understand. Nevertheless, it may take an entire lifetime to integrate it, to infuse it into our own lives.

In the tradition of Zen dialogues, although the questioner may use such imagery as trees and leaves, he is actually asking about Mind. As you can see, there are many, many trees on this Dai Bosatsu Mountain. When we are immature, we are like green trees in the Spring. We have many leaves: thoughts, ideas, opinions, emotional reactions, psychological problems, and so on. But after sitting five, six days, as you have noticed yourselves, such leaves are dropping away, becoming fewer and fewer. But we have not yet dropped all of them. We still have the attachment to, or expectation of, or ideas about so-called enlightenment. Or we still puzzle about the problems of life and death, sickness, and old age.

Anyhow, this monk is asking Master Ummon, "What will happen when thoughts, ideas, opinions, emotional reactions, psychological problems, attachments, expectations, life, death, sickness, and old age all fall away and our minds become bare?"

What will happen?

Ummon's answer in Japanese is *tairo kimpu*. Literally, *tai* means "body" and *ro* means "manifestation" or "revelation." *Kimpu* means "golden wind." In order to inject Ummon's spirit into English-speaking students more directly, I believe that it is better just to translate *tairo kimpu* as "golden wind."

According to Chinese thought, the universe is composed of five elements: wood, fire, earth, gold, and water. Each season is associated with one of these elements: spring is wood, summer is fire, winter is water and autumn is gold. The element earth is attached to all four seasons. Golden wind is the autumn wind and the autumn wind is a fresh, lucid, and cool wind. Ummon was saying to this monk that life, from morning till evening, when all of these human problems are gone, is like a cool wind blowing through an autumnal forest—all is calm and clear. And this must be one of the most ideal states of mind.

Here I should like to tell you about Ummon's *san-ku*. It is said that each of Ummon's answers functions simultaneously in three ways. *San-ku* implies "three functions." To illustrate these three functions, the following metaphors are used:

1. The cover (the answer) fits the box (the question).
2. The boat (the answer) rocks with the waves (the question).
3. The answer cuts through the streams of delusion (of the questioner).

Now let us see how these *san-ku* apply to Ummon's "Golden Wind."

A monk asked Ummon, "What will happen when the leaves fall and the trees become bare?"
Ummon said, "Golden Wind!"

24

It is obvious that the monk was not interested in trees and leaves. He really wanted to find out about Ummon's state of mind. But the question, "What is your state of mind?" smells too much of Zen. Also, by disguising his real intent, the monk is presenting Ummon with a Dharma challenge.

Because of his unique genius, Ummon was able to see through the monk and his question. Therefore he said, "Golden Wind!" This Golden Wind fits the imagery of falling leaves and bare trees like a cover fits a box. Rocking with the waves of the monk's challenging question, Golden Wind is like a boat rocking with the waves of a storm. Golden Wind blows away the monk's streams of delusions. While all of these three are acting simultaneously within the one answer, Golden Wind, Ummon is also perfectly revealing his own state of mind, thus meeting the monk's Dharma challenge.

The more we study Ummon's answers, the more we are able to appreciate Zen poetry and the state of mind thus revealed.

As I said before, it is relatively easy to intellectually interpret Ummon's Golden Wind, but do not forget that the real aim of zazen lies not with this kind of interpretive explanation. Rather, it lies with the penetration of Golden Wind into our bodies and minds so that someday, although it may take three, four, even five decades, we may be able to mature a similar, if not the same, state of mind as Ummon.

> *Cool wind blows gently through our minds,*
> *No matter what happens!*
> *No matter what happens,*
> *Cool wind blows gently through our minds!*

Dai Bosatsu Zendo Kongo-ji
September 9, 1977

Bodhidharma's Reality

The Blue Rock Collection: Case 1

Introductory Words:

When one sees smoke over the mountains he should quickly know that there is a fire. When one sees horns over a fence he should immediately know that there is an ox. Seeing one thing, at least three matters must become clear. This is such a fundamental tea and rice matter for all Zen students. Cutting off the various strings at once, appearing in the East and disappearing in the West, he is free from all restrictions. How about this! What sort of person acts like this! Look!

The Teisho:

During this sesshin I plan to give the teishos on *The Blue Rock Collection, The Hekigan Roku.* In general, regarding our zazen practice, there is one extremely important matter which I hope you will not only understand but will also keep in your minds all the time. This matter is the difference between *doji no inga* and *iji no inga. Inga* means "cause and effect," *in* is "cause" and *ga* is "effect." *Doji* means "at the time," *do* is "same" and *ji* is "time." *Iji* means "at different times." So sometimes cause and effect appear simultaneously and sometimes cause happens first and effect appears later on. For example, if you are working in the monastery and by some mistake you cut your finger (the cause) the subsequent pain and bleeding (the effect) are immediately apparent. This is *doji no inga.* Now, perhaps another time when you are working around the monastery area you strike some part of your body, say your hip. When it happens you do not immediately feel any pain. But, let us say, after taking a bath in the evening you start to feel the pain. So the cause happened in the morning, but the effect was not noticed until later. This is *iji no inga.*

I am really speaking about this cause and effect matter in connection with zazen practice. In general there are two categories of zazen. One is known as *Mokusho Zen* (Silently Illuminating Zen), and *shikantaza* (just sitting) is its main practice. In the practice of shikantaza, cause and effect appear simultaneously. The sitting is the cause and at the very same time it is also the effect. The other category is called *Kanna Zen*, and koan Zen is its main practice. In this case, cause and effect rarely happen at once. One needs many years of sitting for the time to become ready. Then, suddenly, the effect happens. But to be precise and in order to avoid this kind of analysis or classification, I must say that zazen practice is both the process of cause and effect appearing simultaneously and the process of cause first and effect appearing later.

The shikantaza point of view is that one minute's clear sitting is one minute's clear enlightenment. The koan Zen point of view is that from one minute's intense concentration there will be one minute of concentrated energy accumulation. This one minute of concentrated energy accumulation is no other than one minute of lucid Mind. Little by little, conditions reach maturity and at one point our inner Eye opens. Whichever view we prefer, the plain fact is that zazen, especially clear zazen, is unquestionably the manifestation of Buddha-Dharma or, more precisely, the manifestion of our True Nature. We are here to practice that and to testify to that.

Now about *The Blue Rock Collection*: The golden age of Zen in China flourished during the T'ang Dynasty but was over by the Sung Dynasty. In the Sung Dynasty there lived a genius-poet Zen master who was called Setcho Zenji (977/80–1052). This Setcho selected one hundred koans from among the many that were circulating throughout the Zen monasteries. For each of the selected one hundred koans he composed a verse. It is said that it took Setcho twenty years to compose the one hundred verses. One of my favorite verses goes like this:

> *Overwhelming evening clouds*
> *Gathering in one great mass.*
> *Endlessly arising distant mountains*
> *Blue heaped upon blue.*

Although the verses were composed some one thousand years ago and are now being read in translated form, they still have great inspirational value. It is said that whenever Setcho completed a verse after a great struggle, he would bow on the floor innumerable times and offer it to the patriarchs.

About ninety years after Setcho had died, another genius Zen master was born. His name was Engo Kokugon Zenji (1063–1135). It was this Engo who wrote the introductory remarks for each case, along with short, sharp annotations for each phrase of each koan and verse. Also, for each case he wrote one long commentary. So each case of *The Blue Rock Collection* consists of four parts:

1. The introductory remarks by Engo
2. The main koan compiled by Setcho and annotated by Engo
3. A long teisho-like explanatory commentary by Engo
4. A verse composed by Setcho and annotated by Engo

Now the question is: how did *The Blue Rock Collection* get its name? The story goes that when Master Engo was writing his commentaries and introductory remarks he lived in a temple on Mount Ka (*Kassan* in Japanese). Before Setcho and Engo there had lived another Zen master who was named after that mountain, Kassan. This Master Kassan was once asked, "What is the condition of Kassan?" This question implies two things: the condition of Kassan, the mountain, and the state of mind of Master Kassan, the person. Kassan's reply was:

> *The monkeys carrying their babies*
> *Return to the far side of the blue peaks.*
> *Birds holding flowers in their beaks*
> *Let them fall before the blue rocks.*

Probably the temple where Kassan lived was located near a rocky cliff, like we see in Chinese paintings. In any case, when Master Engo was studying Setcho's one hundred stories he was staying in a room in that temple on Kassan. In that very room there hung a plaque on which were written two Chinese characters: *heki gan* or "blue rock." So after Engo had completed his commentaries, which had taken him over twenty years, looking up at that old calligraphy he decided to name his work *Hekigan Roku*. If something else had been written on that plaque I would not now be speaking about blue rocks. It would be something else. This is the explanation of the origin of the title.

The introductory words to the first koan are: When one sees smoke over the mountain, he should quickly know that there is a fire. When one sees horns over the fence, he should immediately know that there is an ox.

When we Zen students see smoke over the mountains, we should immediately know that there is a fire. Is that a fire from tobacco? Is the smoke from burning trash? Is that smoke from a real fire? These things also should be immediately recognized. Zen students have to learn to quickly grasp the active aspect of Zen, that is, to see the one and discern the many. When one sees horns over a fence, instead of being aware of just an ox, we should know why the ox is here today. This is what I call the active aspect of Zen. When one sees a car coming on Sunday over the bridge, we should be able to discern who is coming and why they are coming. Of course it is important to do quiet, peaceful zazen. But it is equally important to be able to immediately discern two or three things by seeing only one thing. Sometimes our imagination may go too far, causing us trouble. So be careful!

Suppose a person is walking on the street and sees ox excrement. He may say "This is ox excrement," and just continue along. He cannot be a wonderful Zen student—just passing by the dung of an ox. He should have known when it was done, how it will be taken care of, and who will do the cleaning up and when. Perhaps this is why Zen is called a pragmatic and rational teaching. Our feet are on the ground. Since dung is on the street we cannot be only looking up towards heaven. To be high is all right, as long as our feet are on the ground. But if we walk like hydrogen balloons we lose the base of our zazen practice. I have no objection to speaking about "wonderful spirituality," but keep your feet on the ground! "When you see the smoke, you should quickly know that there is a fire. When you see the horns over the fence, you should immediately know that there is an ox."

"Seeing one thing, at least three matters must become clear." Actually it is not just three, but at least ten matters must become clear. In the East meals are sometimes eaten out of four-cornered boxes. So Engo was saying that by seeing one corner we should be able to detect the other three corners. In other words, by seeing one thing, we should have a quick enough mind to be able to know the whole matter. Confucius said: "If one cannot see the rest of the three after seeing one of the four, he is not worthy enough to become my student."

To continue with the introductory words. ". . . such a fundamental tea and rice matter . . ." "Tea and rice matter" perhaps does not make much sense to you but in the East, every day, we eat rice and drink tea. Because we are in the West perhaps we should call it "a bread and butter matter." Seeing one, knowing at least ten—this is the fundamental bread and butter matter for all Zen students. Now, this is wonderful!

Some of us have different notions about Zen and zazen. Some believe that to do Zen practice it is necessary to seclude themselves from human relations, from noisy society, from polluted air, and so on, in order to become enlightened. This is not bad, of course, but it is what I would call passive or selfish Zen. We go into seclusion in order to revive ourselves so that when we return to human society we will know how to live, how not to be deceived by others, and how to be creative and constructive. It is important for us to know that we cannot escape from human society. We can only absent ourselves for a while. This is what we are learning in sesshin—such a fundamental bread and butter matter! We are learning to "cut off the various strings at once."

> However inexhaustible all delusions are,
> We vow to extinguish them all.

So "cutting off the various strings at once" means cutting through the various delusions at once. But this doesn't mean a thing; it doesn't have any impact. And what kind of strings do we have? Let me explain it like this. Sometimes we become unhappy, sometimes we feel self-pity, sometimes we feel miserable. There are various reasons for these negative feelings. We should try to dig them out, one by one, even though normally we try to avoid such confrontations. These reasons are the "various strings." And how do we cut them off? We cannot cut them off in the way that we cut real strings, that is, with scissors. It is not as simple as that. Although these beads of mine are held together by a strong silk string, if I were to use them every day, year after year, one day the string would break all by itself. In the same way, our many strings cannot be cut at once by kensho. But they can be cut through with daily zazen; dedicated, patient sitting, month after month, year after year. And one day, iji no inga! When I rub my beads (the cause) they become shinier and shinier, the string becomes weaker and weaker and, at one point, the string breaks all by itself (the effect). So there is no instant Zen practice. There is only patient practice.

"Cutting off the various strings at once, appearing in the East and disappearing in the West, he is free from all restrictions." "Free from all restrictions"—this part can be very misleading. We have many restrictions and rules for sesshin and for everyday life in the monastery. But these rules are for the purpose of attaining freedom. "Appearing in the East and disappearing in the West"—freedom. In our present state of mind, we have to pass through the gate of restrictions in order to be truly free from restrictions. America is a free country. Yet we know that there aren't very many free men and women. As far as I am concerned, what we are aiming for is to become free men and women living in a free country. America is a free country—freedom of speech, freedom of faith, freedom of everything. But we cannot be free from ourselves. The gate of restrictions, rules, and regulations may be very uncomfortable—don't move, don't stand up, don't smile, don't talk, don't, don't, don't . . .! Everything seems to be don't, don't, don't . . .! But this is the way that tradition teaches us to become free. True freedom!

"Cutting off the various strings at once, appearing in the East and disappearing in the West"—free from all restrictions!

"How about this! What sort of person acts like this! Look!" Thus ends Engo's introductory words and we are now ready to appreciate the actions of a free man.

The Koan:
   Attention!
   The Chinese Emperor Wu asked Bodhidharma, "What is the First Holy Reality?"
   Bodhidharma answered, "In this whole universe there is nothing to be labeled the First Holy Reality."

The emperor inquired, *"Who are you?"*

Bodhidharma answered, *"I know not."*

The emperor did not understand this answer. Bodhidharma then crossed the river and went to the north.

Afterwards the emperor repeated this dialogue to Shiko. Shiko asked, *"Does His Majesty know this man?"*

The emperor replied, *"I know not."*

Shiko said, *"He is really a Kanzeon Bodhisattva, a messenger of Buddha who came to teach you."*

Hearing this, the emperor was deeply regretful and wanted to call Bodhidharma back. Shiko said, *"Even if you were to send all of your people to the north to fetch Bodhidharma, he will never come back."*

The Verse:

> *Holy Reality! Emptiness!*
> *Who is this that confronts me?*
> *"I do not know."*
> *It was because of this that in the dark*
> * he crossed the river.*
> *How can the growth of thorns and*
> * entangling briars be avoided?*
> *Even if all the people of the land*
> * pursue him,*
> *He will never return.*
> *Eternally and everlastingly regret it in*
> * vain.*
> *Stop! Discontinue the regret!*
> *Cool breeze over the whole universe!*
> *How limitless it is!*

The Teisho:

All Zen students know that there are two schools of Zen Buddhism: Rinzai and Soto. But there are also two kinds of Zen: Nyorai and Soshi. Literally, *nyorai* means "the Tathagata" and *soshi* means "patriarch." As far as the names of types of Zen go, to speak of Patriarch Zen and Tathagata Zen is rather confusing. I will tell you a story which I hope will make the difference clearer.

About one hundred years ago in Japan there was a young traveling monk. Before coming to the monastery he had studied Sanskrit, Pali, Tibetan, and all the Buddhist philosophers including Nagarjuna. His teacher had finally said to him, "I have nothing more to teach you. You should now go to a Zen monastery."

So this monk went to a Zen monastery, but because of his pride and because of his knowledge of Buddhism, he was not particularly enthusiastic about doing zazen. One summer he became sick and had to stay in one of the rooms which was set up like an infirmary. And it so happened that a senior monk also became sick and went to this sick room. Neither monk was seriously ill. One day this young man asked the senior monk "I understand that there is a Nyorai Zen and a Soshi Zen. Would you be good enough to tell me the difference between the two?"

The older monk replied, "All right, but before I do so, I have heard that you are an expert on Buddhist philosophy. I should therefore like to hear you give a discourse on the *Heart Sutra*."

The young monk consented and on the following day he began his talk on the *Heart Sutra*. In the customary fashion, he would read a phrase and explain its meaning. After a while he came to the part which goes: "*Shiki soku ze ku, ku soku ze shiki.*" "Form (material) is emptiness, emptiness is form."

Since it was summer, while he was speaking the young monk was cooling himself with a fan. The old one said, "Wait! Is your fan *shiki* (material) or *ku* (non-material or emptiness)?"

The young one naturally said, "Of course this is *shiki*, this is material."

The old monk then said, "All right, I take your statement and I take your fan. Now give me ku (emptiness)!"

And it is at this point that the intelligent young fellow could not utter even a single word. Immediately the old monk said, "This is Soshi Zen. What you know already is Nyorai Zen."

Nyorai Zen is intellectual Zen, so to speak. Soshi Zen is more dynamic, spontaneous, and creative. It is more vivid, more alive, and non-conceptual. The actualization of Soshi Zen is what we are aiming for in our practice. Coming to this zendo is not like attending a class at the New School for Social Research. There we can learn Nyorai Zen. Here we practice Soshi Zen.

When one sees smoke over the mountain, he should quickly know what is happening, how it was caused, and how to act accordingly. This cannot be learned through Nyorai Zen conceptions. On the other hand, in a deeper sense, Nyorai Zen and Soshi Zen do overlap. In their writings, Nyogen Senzaki and Hakuun Yasutani Roshi exhibit Nyorai Zen tendencies. Soen Roshi is just appropriate for this koan, "appearing in the East and disappearing in the West," cancelling appointments only to suddenly appear. He is certainly a Soshi Zen master. This is a not a matter of good or bad—it is just the way it is. Rinzai himself was a typical Soshi Zen master. Our Rinzai Zen lineage has more Soshi Zen tendencies. So naturally we do more zazen and use the keisaku. Sometimes our practice seems sort of rough, but by means of this roughness, we are trying to go beyond what we can learn from books and lectures.

"All right, I accept this shiki but give me ku." You can give that old monk ku as easily as you can give him shiki. "Form is emptiness, emptiness is form." This fan, which I am holding, is easily recognizable as form. But as for the ku, the emptiness—how can you give it to me? While you are thinking about it, I'll just fan myself and enjoy the breeze.

Everything is Mu—whether we understand it or not; whether we are sleepy or not; whether we are deluded or not—everything is Mu and everything is *sunyata* (ku, emptiness). "All right, I take shiki, now give me ku!" At this moment most of the Nyorai Zen students must stop to think, "Well, what shall I do? What is the most appropriate gift? In what manner shall I present ku?" During this hesitation, if they were soldiers, the enemy would surely take advantage, and they would be shot and killed.

Intellectual Zen cannot cover that one moment of hesitation. And in fact, life is a continuation of moments—moment after moment, moment after moment . . . . Most of the moments are, fortunately, quiet moments. But there are many moments which are not, and you have to make immediate decisions. It is at this time that Soshi Zen, which we are practicing, which we are trying to master, shows its potency.

So, back to today's koan. "Attention!" We hear this command so often that we no longer pay attention to "Attention!" But here it is a key word, "Attention!"

Bodhidharma (d. 532) was the twenty-eighth patriarch from Shakyamuni Buddha. He came to China in 520 A.D. He is really the first one to begin the mysterious movement of Buddha-Dharma from East to West. There were twenty-eight generations of teachers in China and twenty-eight generations of teachers in Japan, and now in America. . .! Why twenty-eight? No one knows.

It is said that when Bodhidharma came to China he was already over one hundred years old and that it had taken him three years to travel by boat from India to China. When he landed he went straight to see Emperor Wu, who was a very faithful Buddhist. He had built many temples and had printed *sutras* and *shastras*. This emperor had evidently done all kinds of work for the Buddha-Dharma expecting to accumulate certain kinds of merit and virtue. So it is said that the first question the emperor asked of Bodhidharma was, "What kind of merit can I get?" To this Bodhidharma said, "No virtue whatsoever, no merit at all!" That is to say, "Fundamentally speaking, no virtue whatsoever, no merit at all!" Nothing to gain, nothing to lose!

And the next question that the emperor asked of Bodhidharma was, "What is the First Holy Reality?"

Bodhidharma answered, "In this whole universe," in the boundless universe, "there is nothing to be called first," or second, "nothing to be called holy," or unholy. This part of the koan should be clarified in dokusan.

Incidentally, recently a book called *The Sound of One Hand* was published. This book is a collection of over two hundred koans and their "answers." So if you are interested you should get it. In a way I am glad that such a strange book appears. Actually there are no answers, as such, to koans. If a student is assigned to a specific koan, he may go back to his room and look up the answer in the book. If it exactly matches

35

his teacher's answer, he can pass through the koan. But even after two or three hundred or more of such answers he will still be unable to get either Soshi Zen or Nyorai Zen. The ideal Soshi Zen answer must be spontaneous, dynamic, creative, constantly changing . . . it can never be printed.

The emperor asked, "Who are you?"

Bodhidharma answered, "I know not."

The sun rises from the east and sets in the west. Why? Because the earth is rotating around the sun. Why? Because of the physical laws of the universe. Why! I don't know! So even with modern scientific excellence and years of research we still do not know the primary cause of the universe. We think that we know quite a few things, but it is very little compared to the great amount of things which we do not know. As Goethe's Faust says:

> I've studied now Philosophy
> And Jurisprudence, Medicine,
> And even, alas! Theology
> All through and through with ardor keen!
> Here now I stand, poor fool, and see
> I'm just as wise as formerly.
> I'm called a Master, even Doctor too,
> And now I've nearly ten years through
> Pulled my students by their noses to and fro
> And up and down, across, about
> And see there's nothing we can know!

The emperor could not understand Bodhidharma's "I don't know," so Bodhidharma gave up on him and crossed the river to go to the north, to a temple called Shorin-ji. It is there, it is said, that he sat in zazen for nine years.

Let us keep in our minds that we do zazen here, today, to master Soshi Zen, Patriarch Zen, dynamic Zen, vivid Zen, positive Zen, unintellectual Zen, spontaneous Zen, elegant Zen, and some other words.

Speaking about here, today in the *Song of Zazen* by Master Hakuin we come across this passage: "This very place is the Lotus Land of Purity." This does not mean that Dai Bosatsu Zendo is a complete Lotus Land of Purity. Rather it is through our practice that every place, even in the noisy city in the middle of complicated personal problems, becomes the Lotus Land of Purity. It is perhaps almost impossible for us to feel this way all the time. Still, this is one of the goals. This is why we go to sesshin, time and again. Each time we attend a sesshin, we feel more, more, and more that "this place is the Lotus Land of Purity."

To continue with Bodhidharma, the First Patriarch in China:

The emperor asked, "Who are you?"

Bodhidharma answered, "I know not."

Most of you have seen Master Hakuin's portrait of Bodhidharma with his long beard and piercing eyes. And there above it are two Chinese characters describing so simply the essence of the painting. The calligraphy reads: *Fu Shiki*, "I know not." This is the essence of Zen.

One caution: when Bodhidharma said, "I know not" or when Faust said, "And see there's nothing we can know" or when Soyen Shaku in San Francisco in 1905 said:

I have studied Buddhism for more than forty years and have preached the teaching here and there. But only very recently have I begun to understand it. Now, I understand that what I have understood is that after all I do not understand anything.

you may wonder, "If the answer is so clear, 'I don't know,' why do I have to strive with this pain?" It takes as many years as we spend to learn something as it does to reach the point where we can truthfully say, "After all, we do not know." This is so difficult for us to say. We can say very carelessly, "Oh, I don't know," but something else is involved. We think we do know, we think that we are able to know. Being trained in "I don't know" is positive. It is not at all negative. From "I don't know" there is growth. From "I don't know" many things can really sprout.

So this is why we strive. This is the reason for enduring pain. We

37

don't know why we are sitting; we don't know why we have to suffer the pain; we don't know; we are unable to know; we don't know why. And yet we are not stupid. There is some Dharma wave or karmic force in each of us. Just ride it like a surfboard!

But for koan study, Emperor Wu's "Who are you" and Bodhidharma's "I don't know" are so subtle. It can only be presented one to one, from heart to heart. Therefore dokusan is needed. You strike the bell, come into the dokusan room, bow, and thoroughly respond to this koan with your body and mind. This is the way that the transmission of the Dharma is carried on.

My teacher, Soen Roshi, used to say to the monks in his monastery, Ryutaku-ji, in order to encourage them, "Look, you monks! What is the matter with you? Don't worry about koan study. Once you really break through and get enlightenment, come to me with your paper and pencil. I will give you all the answers. You can just copy them down."

"Afterwards, when the emperor told Shiko about his dialogue with Bodhidharma, Shiko politely asked, " 'Does His Majesty know this man?' "

"The emperor replied, 'I know not.' "

This "I know not" is quite different from Bodhidharma's "I know not." Appreciate the difference! There is a Zen saying:

A tenth of an inch's difference
And heaven and earth are set apart.

"Shiko said, 'He is really a Kanzeon Bodhisattva.' "

Often people ask, "Is Kanzeon a male or is Kanzeon a female?" If we consider Kanzeon Bodhisattva as a fixed entity, either man or woman, Kanzeon Bodhisattva loses its miraculous, mysterious power. It is neither man or woman. KANZEON! It is just the personification of the compassionate aspect of Buddha nature.

Anyhow," . . . Kanzeon Bodhisattva, a messenger of the Buddha."

Hearing this, Emperor Wu, a faithful Buddhist, was so astonished. "Aha! And I missed my chance!" It is said that he tried to call Bodhidharma back, but Shiko said, "Even if you were to send all of your

people to the north to fetch Bodhidharma, he will never come back."
  Why?
  To finish with Bodhidharma, there is one point in the verse which
is particularly related:

> *Cool breeze over the whole universe!*
> *How limitless it is!*

The transmission of Buddha-Dharma was accomplished by Bodhidharma. But even today, by this Beecher Lake, the transmission is
still continuing. Cool breeze in summer; waves move along the lake;
birds sing in the trees; snowflakes in winter; beautiful moon in August.
So the transmission of Buddha-Dharma began even prior to heaven
and earth. It is nonsense to say that Bodhidharma brought Zen from
India to China, that Eisai Zenji brought Rinzai Zen from China to
Japan, that Dogen brought Soto Zen from China to Japan, that Soyen
Shaku and some others brought it from Japan to America. It has already been transmitted even before human beings began speaking
about something called Zen. But at the same time, without Bodhi-
dharma's physical coming from India to China, Zen Buddhism would
have not developed in China, and without Eisai Zenji's and Dogen
Zenji's voyages to China, Zen Buddhism would have not grown in
Japan, and so it is true that without Soyen Shaku, D.T. Suzuki, Nyogen Senzaki, and some other teachers' great efforts, perhaps Beecher
Lake would have remained merely Beecher Lake, instead of the site of
Dai Bosatsu Zendo. Some transmission effort is necessary. But even if
all the people of the land had pursued him, he would have never come
back. Indeed, he need not come back because he has always been
there, "even prior to heaven and earth." And this is true whether you
understand it or not!

Dai Bosatsu Zendo Kongo-ji
June 29–July 1, 1975

Joshu's Mu

The Gateless Gate: Case 1

The Koan:

A monk asked Joshu, "Has a dog Buddha nature or not?"
Joshu said, "Mu!"

Mumon's Comment:

To realize Zen one has to pass through the barrier of the Patriarchs.
Enlightenment follows when the road of thinking ceases. If you do not
pass the barrier of the Patriarchs, or if your road of thinking does not
cease, then no matter what you think, no matter what you do, you are like
a tangling ghost. You may ask, "What is the barrier of the Patriarchs?"
This one word, "Mu," is it. This is the barrier of Zen. If you pass
through it, you will see Joshu face to face. Then you can walk hand-in-
hand with the whole line of Patriarchs. Is this not a pleasant thing to do?
If you want to pass this barrier, you must work through every bone in
your body, through every pore of your skin. You must become filled with
the question, "What is Mu?" Carry it with you day and night. Do not
believe that it is the common negative syllable meaning "nothing." It is
not nothingness, the opposite of existence. If you really want to pass this
barrier, you should feel as if you had a hot iron ball embedded in your
throat. You can neither swallow it nor spit it out. Then your previous
lesser knowledge disappears. Like a fruit ripening in season, your subjec-
tivity and objectivity naturally become one. You are like a dumb man
who has had a dream. Your ego shell is crushed and you can shake the
heaven and move the earth. You are like a great warrior holding a sharp
sword. If a Buddha stands in your way, cut him down. If a Patriarch
blocks your way, kill him. You will be free from birth and death. You
will be able to enter any world as if it were your own playground. I will
tell you how to do this with this koan. Just concentrate your whole energy

into this Mu, and do not allow any disruptions to sway you. When you enter this Mu and there are no disruptions, your attainment will be like a burning candle illuminating the whole universe.

The Verse:

> *Has a dog Buddha nature?*
> *This question is the expression of Truth, itself.*
> *If you say, "Yes,"*
> *Or if you say, "No,"*
> *You lose your Buddha nature.*

The Teisho:

Since this is the very first day of our first kessei (one hundred days of uninterrupted Zen training in a monastery), I thought it better to start our study of *The Gateless Gate* from the very beginning. We will continue its study during the next one hundred days so that our understanding of Zen Buddhism, that is, our understanding of Mind, may become clearer.

Before I begin speaking about Mu, I must mention a few other important matters. Some of you have attended sesshin many times. But today, let us consider ourselves as beginners, not acquainted with the various matters connected with Zen practice. To understand Zen practice, we must first of all realize that body, breath, and mind are to be regarded as one inseparable unit. At the same time, we must also keep in our minds that body, breath, and mind belong to separate, distinct categories. This time, let me speak about "body." "Body" implies many things. First, "body" refers to your zazen posture, sitting on a cushion with your eyes open. Another body condition is what I call "gassho body." One kind of gassho is just putting your hands together in a sort of absent-minded way. But there is another gassho—you truly put your palms together, without separating your fingers. Not only do you feel good when you gassho in this manner, but also if someone happens to look at you, he can get inspiration from your sincere gassho.

Another important body condition is your posture while doing kinhin. Some of us put our hands on our chests and some of us place our fists way down, below the lower abdomen. And some of us walk with our hands placed somewhere in between. The best place to put your hands while doing kinhin is above the area of your navel. If someone is holding his hands in the right way, he is helping to create a slightly more intensive atmosphere. This is his contribution. Walking speaks almost everything about our mental condition. If you have to go to a neurologist, the first thing that he'll ask you to do is to walk back and forth in a straight line. Evidently, to walk straight, step by step, is not such an easy task. Also, if someone is looking around during kinhin, not only is he not able to do his own zazen, but he is also destroying the others' concentration.

To continue with body conditions, let me speak about holding the sutra book. It is a very tiny matter, but it is just such tiny matters that are important for us to focus upon. So hold the sutra book with two hands at eye level, keeping your back straight. In this way, you can do chanting zazen.

As long as I am speaking about sutra books, I should like to say a few things about chanting. Your voice, being another body condition, makes chanting another form of zazen. In the morning we begin the services by chanting:

ATTA-DIPA
VIHARATHA
ATTA-SARANA
ANANNA-SARANA
DHAMMA-DIPA
DHAMMA-SARANA
ANANNA-SARANA

Dwell!
You are the Light itself
Rely on yourself
Do not rely on others
The Dharma is the Light
Rely on the Dharma
Do not rely on anything other than the Dharma

This Pali verse, it is said, are the actual words of Shakyamuni himself. It came from his own lips in Pali, the language spoken during his lifetime. Although it is a simple verse, it is extremely important. At the same time it has some special musical effect. It creates a kind of religious feeling.

Next we chant *Vandana* and *Tissarana*. These are very important Buddhist gathas.

Vandana

NAMO TASSA
BHAGAVATO ARAHATO
SAMMA SAMBUDILASSA

Homage to the Buddha,
The Venerable One,
The Enlightened One,
The Supremely Awakened One!

Tissarana

BUDDHAM SARANAM GACCHAMI
DHAMMAN SARANAM GACCHAMI
SANGHAM SARANAM GACCHAMI

I take refuge in the Buddha
I take refuge in the Dharma
I take refuge in the Sangha

You should memorize both the original Pali and its English meaning, so that while you are chanting you will be able to know what you are chanting.

Next we recite *Purification:*

All the evil karma ever committed by me since of old,
On account of my beginningless greed, anger, and folly,
Born of my body, mouth, and thought—
I now confess and purify them all.

Since this is English, at least we can immediately know what we are

43

saying. But it is not enough just to know, we must chant with feeling.
After *Purification* we chant *Opening This Dharma*:

> *This Dharma,*
> *Incomparably profound and minutely subtle,*
> *Is hardly met with*
> *Even in hundreds of thousands of millions of eons.*
> *We now can see this,*
> *Listen to this,*
> *Accept and hold this.*
> *May we completely understand and actualize*
> *This Tathagata's true meaning.*

After the *Heart Sutra* and the *Great Light Dharani*, the *ino* or sutra leader chants the dedication while we sit with our palms together in gassho. Although we are not chanting, we should be with it at least in spirit. The dedication begins:

> *Buddha nature pervades the whole universe,*
> *Revealing right here, now . . .*

What does it mean when we say that Buddha nature pervades the whole universe, revealing right here, now? When we understand this thoroughly we may consider ourselves graduate students of the school of Zen Buddhism.

At the very end of the dedication, the leader has been chanting:

> *Past, Present, Future,*
> *All Buddhas, Bodhisattvas.*
> *Let True Dharma continue.*
> *Universal Sangha relation.*
> *International Dai Bosatsu Zendo Kongo-ji*
> *Become complete.*

But now, let us eliminate "Kongo-ji" from the dedication. Up until the Fourth of July 1976, the completion of this monastery, International Dai Bosatsu Zendo Kongo-ji, was our prayer. But now, at last, this

Kongo-ji is completed, so it is not necessary to include it anymore. But how about International Dai Bosatsu Zendo? International Dai Bosatsu Zendo, in order that its completion occur, must be found in every place. If there is a zendo in the Philippines, Rumania, Portugal, Czechoslovakia, then they are all International Dai Bosatsu Zendos. As long as there is a black cushion and someone to sit on it, that itself is International Dai Bosatsu Zendo. So International Dai Bosatsu Zendo cannot be completed with the construction of a building. Actually, it will never be completed.

It is just like the vows: however innumerable all beings are, we vow to save them all; there are innumerable, inexhaustible delusions, but we vow to extinguish them all. We are trying, just trying, although these are, in a sense, contradictory statements. But it is this very trying to accomplish the vows that brings to some of us the great meaning of existence. There is nothing which is wasteful. And there is nothing which is not accomplished each moment. The moment we say *SHUJO MUHEN SEI GAN DO* (however innumerable all beings are, we vow to save them all), that is the very moment that all beings are saved. When we chant, *SHUJO MUHEN SEI GAN DO*, we should do so full of pep, full of energy. In the same way, International Dai Bosatsu Zendo will be completed, but not in the ordinary sense of completion. When we realize that our vow to save all sentient beings on this earth means to give up trying to change other people's personalities, and rather to accept them as they are, at that moment International Dai Bosatsu Zendo will be completed.

Now we are ready for "Joshu's Mu":

Joshu Jushin Zenji (778–897) was one of the most outstanding Zen masters of the T'ang Dynasty. One day a traveling monk came to him and asked, "Has a dog Buddha nature or not?" To this question, Joshu replied, "Mu!"

Let us begin with Buddha nature. In Buddhism, all beings, even all inanimate objects, have Buddha nature. But here the word "have" is misleading. It sounds as if we can possess something apart from ourselves. Actually, whatever each thing consists of, that totality is called Buddha nature. So each cell of our bodies is Buddha nature and our whole body itself is also Buddha nature. The same is true for this world

45

and all the things in it. This whole world is Buddha nature and, even on a larger scale, the whole universe with the stars and solar systems—the totality of the universe is called Buddha nature. Thus we say, "Buddha nature pervades the whole universe . . ." In short, I am nothing but Buddha nature; he is nothing but Buddha nature; it is nothing but Buddha nature; so on and so forth. Despite this obvious fact, the monk asked, "Does a dog have Buddha nature or not?" To this, Joshu replied, "Mu!"

Mu literally means "no." But remember this important point: we are not studying semantics; we are practicing zazen. Avoid the intellectualization of Mu and Buddha nature. Joshu was just giving us another name for Buddha nature that is Mu!

I will tell you an interesting story which starts with confusion but ends with realization. In the *Heart Sutra* there is a phrase, *MU GEN NI BI ZES SHIN NI*, normally translated as "no eye, ear, nose, tongue, body, mind," as Mu literally means "no." When Kyozan was a young monk he touched his face and thought, "I do have eyes, ears, nose, and tongue. Why then does the *Heart Sutra* say that there are none?" This became Kyozan's most pressing question, but he could find nobody capable of answering it. He held that question all the time while his zazen became more and more mature. One day, while on a pilgrimage, he was walking along a road, wearing straw sandals and thinking to himself, *MU GEN NI BI ZES SHIN NI*. This time, because of his zazen maturity, Mu as Buddha nature and Mu as "no" became interfused. As he was walking he stubbed his toe on a stone. It was extremely painful and he began to bleed. Suddenly he was able to truly feel *MU GEN* (eyes), *MU NI* (ears), *MU BI* (nose), *MU ZETSU* (tongue), *MU SHIN* (body), *MU NI* (mind) and *MU TOE*! It's not that he had no toe, but that very toe itself was Mu. Thus did Kyozan come to understand *MU GEN NI BI ZES SHIN NI*.

From the Mu point of view, that is, from the Buddha nature point of view, that is, from the Awakened point of view, this world, this universe is the fully blossomed Buddha nature. In other words, everything, tangible or not, visual or not, ugly or beautiful, life and death, is Mu. Why then do we need to say this? Why do we need to realize this? It is simply because we have a one-sided view of reality—the existential view that all things are separate and different—and we think that this view of reality is the whole view.

How should we practice Mu? Mumon's comment describes the practice very well. It requires tremendous attention. It needs ceaseless concentration. It asks for dynamic sitting.

MU-U-U-U! MU-U-U-U! MU-U-U-U!

Day and night—MU-MU-MU! Become MU! Forget time, forget environment, forget self—MU-MU-MU! Put aside uncertainty— MU-MU-MU! If you do exactly what I have just said, as Master Hakuin tells us:

Even if you miss striking the ground,
You will never miss realizing your Buddha nature.

Mumon's verse:

Has a dog Buddha nature?
This question is the expression of Truth, itself.
If you say, "Yes,"
Or if you say, "No,"
You lose your Buddha nature.

The question itself, "Has a dog Buddha nature," is the expression of Buddha nature. Great laughter is the expression of Buddha nature. A scream is the expression of Buddha nature. A smile is the expression of Buddha nature. Tears are the expression of Buddha nature. Even if you do say, "Yes" or "No," you actually can never lose it. But if you say only "Yes," opposed to "No," you are expressing only fifty percent of the Truth. If you say only "No," opposed to "Yes," you are still expressing only fifty percent of the Truth.

Sit with Mu and do your very best!

Dai Bosatsu Zendo Kongo-ji
September 5, 1976

47

Hakuin's Rohatsu Exhortation

The First Night:

Master Hakuin said:

"It is essential for you, a student of Dharma who practices zazen, first of all to sit down on a thick cushion in full lotus posture, loosen your robe and belt, straighten your spine, and then calm your body and mind. Then begin to count your breath, from one to ten, in taut silence. To enter deep samadhi this is incomparably the best way.

"As you fill up your hara with zazen energy, start working on your koan with an intensive mind, cutting through all thoughts. If you continue to practice zazen day after day without cease, even if you should miss striking the ground, you cannot fail to experience kensho. Don't you want that?

"Do your best!"

The Teisho:

Every evening during Rohatsu Sesshin I read this *Rohatsu Exhortation* by Hakuin Ekaku Zenji (1686–1769), but today I am going to say a few things about the first section. Evidently, this talk was given casually by Master Hakuin during a Rohatsu Sesshin. He just came into the zendo and spontaneously said something. One of his students memorized the main points and later wrote them down. Almost no comment is needed, but I shall read it and give a comment from time to time. Listen—listen with your hara!

"It is essential for you, a student of Dharma who practices zazen, first of all to sit down on a thick cushion in full lotus posture, loosen your robe and belt, straighten your spine, and then calm your body and mind." If we sit in full lotus and straighten our bodies, there is no other choice but for our bodies and minds to calm down. Even if some of you cannot sit in full lotus, don't be discouraged. To sit in full lotus is not as crucial for zazen as keeping a straight spine. This is one of the secrets of zazen.

As you can see, right now my back is not straight. Sometimes I sit this way deliberately so that, because of my habit of sitting straight, in the middle of zazen my body may become frustrated. This frustration forces me to erect my spine. In this way I do not need to use unnatural physical pressure to keep my back straight at the beginning of each sitting. Due to this gradually erected spine, my back never feels stiff and my breath goes smoothly and regularly. I feel as though my body is like a bathtub drain through which all the dirty water flows out.

Now, how do we prepare ourselves for zazen posture? First cross your legs in a way so that your knees touch the cushion. Stretch your thighs by pulling your knees away from your body. Then lift your buttocks off the cushion (if necessary you may use your hands to support your body) and stretch each buttock apart as much as possible. Keeping your buttocks stretched apart, lower your body back onto the cushion. Now you are well prepared. At this point it is not essential to keep your spine perfectly erect. Then begin to count your breath from one to ten. As you continue zazen, you will feel a great urge to straighten your back. "Taut silence" and "deep samadhi" will come all by themselves.

Some of you think that counting the breath is a practice for beginners and not for advanced students. This is not so. The key point of breath-counting practice is not the counting; rather, it is to enter a condition where the breath flows smoothly, with no interruption of thoughts and without missing the count. This is difficult to master. Through breath-counting practice we realize how many unnecessary and uncontrollable thoughts we have. So everyone needs to perfect their breath-counting practice.

"As you fill up your hara with zazen energy, start working on your koan with an intensive mind, cutting through all thoughts." If we do zazen in the way that I have just described, the area of the lower abdomen, the hara, will be filled with what Master Hakuin calls "zazen energy." This zazen energy is called *chi* in Chinese and *ki* in Japanese. Hara-ly speaking, zazen energy makes us as light as a balloon, yet very firm. When the bell rings to mark the end of a zazen period, we may be surprised how quickly the time passed. We are so comfortable that we don't want to stand up.

". . . Start working on your koan . . ." A koan is not a puzzle wanting a solution. It is used as a kind of aid, helping you to *become* koan samadhi. Although the short chant Na Mu Dai Bosa is not a dialogue, we can use it as a koan. Ceaseless chanting of Na Mu Dai Bosa leads to becoming Na Mu Dai Bosa itself. When Na Mu Dai Bosa is condensed, it becomes Mu-u-u-u . . . and when we continue that Mu-u-u-u, we will enter into a condition where "concentration" is no longer needed. The Mind is like Master Hakuin describes it:

> *How boundless the cleared sky of samadhi!*
> *How transparent the perfect moonlight of the Fourfold Wisdom!*
> *At this moment what more need we seek?*
> *As the Truth eternally reveals itself,*
> *This very place is the Lotus Land of Purity,*
> *This very body is the Body of the Buddha.*

This condition is expediently called shikantaza. So we cannot immediately, at the beginning of each period of zazen, start to practice shikantaza, as such.

Most people, when they hear that there is a practice called "koan study" and a practice called "shikantaza," conclude that these are two different things. This a delusion. Get rid of it. Koan study and shikantaza are the same thing. This is very important to understand, especially for American Zen students. Soto Zen should not be pitted against Rinzai Zen and vice versa. One is not better than the other. To pass hundreds of koans is no great accomplishment. We must eliminate the idea that there are two different kinds of zazen.

When you sit with the koan Mu, and sit with great intensity, having no expectations of "getting kensho," this is what I call "shikan-Mu." Nothing but Mu, JUST MU. This practice is perfect for Americans who have not yet completely molded their understanding of Zen into two separate forms, that is, Soto and Rinzai or so-called passive and active Zen. Shikan-Mu practice fuses together the most important functions of "passive" and "active" zazen. Repeating Mu again and again, with each breath, intensifies and clarifies the mind, while, at the same time, shikan, or "just sitting," takes away the distracting pressure to attain kensho. Shikan-Mu leads into pure shikantaza. Mu acts as an adherent—it helps us to stick to it so that we can continue with intensity. After all, the Dharma will take care of us. No rush!

In the Rinzai tradition of Zen Buddhist practice, it is generally understood that there are seventeen hundred koans to master in order to complete the training. In my opinion, ideally, the best way to enter koan study is to do Mu, then shikan-Mu, then shikantaza, then readiness of time, then self-realization, then, finally, begin koan study. If these steps are followed, the study of all seventeen hundred koans is entirely unnecessary.

The other day I was talking with Professor Masao Abe, a well-known Buddhist scholar who is now lecturing at Princeton University. He asked me what kind of zazen we do here at Dai Bosatsu Zendo. Since he has been visiting various universities and Zen centers in America, he was quite curious to know. When I explained to him about shikan-Mu, he said, "I am so pleased to hear about that, since there are so many junk koans and so much sleeping shikantaza."

Getting back to Master Hakuin: "If you continue to practice zazen day after day without cease, even if you should miss striking the ground, you cannot fail to experience kensho. Don't you want that? Do your best!"

Strictly speaking, we often deceive ourselves about sesshin. It sounds good to say that we are attending Rohatsu Sesshin to commemorate Buddha's enlightenment, that we sit strongly and intensely for seven days with little time for rest and sleep. But how many minutes a day are we really doing zazen? Are we really practicing zazen day after day without cease? And if we do fail to experience kensho, we have ready all kinds of explanations to justify to ourselves why we didn't do good zazen. We never exhaust our supply of skillful rationalizations.

So, as long as we have an ideal place, ideal time, ideal togetherness, let us do exactly what Master Hakuin suggests. Then we will be able to say, "Yes, Master Hakuin, you are quite right, this very body is the Body of the Buddha. Yes, Master Hakuin, you are quite right, this very place is the Lotus Land of Purity. Yes, Master Hakuin, you are quite right, how boundless the cleared sky of samadhi, how transparent the perfect moonlight of the Fourfold Wisdom! At this moment, I don't need any more. JUST THIS . . ."

Let's do our best. Let's do our very best.

Dai Bosatsu Zendo Kongo-ji
December 4, 1977

Hyakujo's Fox

The Gateless Gate: Case 2

The Koan:

Whenever Master Hyakujo gave teisho, an old man would come and sit with the monks. When the monks withdrew after the teisho, so would the old man. But one day he remained behind.

Master Hyakujo asked him, "Who are you standing before me?"

The old man replied, "I am not a human being. Long ago, in the days of Kasho Buddha, I was the head of this monastery. One day, one of the monks asked me, 'Does the enlightened man fall into causation?' I said that he does not. Because of this, I was reborn as a fox five hundred times. Now, I beg of you! Please give me the turning words so that I may be emancipated from this fox existence. Does the enlightened man fall into causation?"

Master Hyakujo said, "The enlightened man is not deceived by causation."

Upon hearing these words, the old man was immediately enlightened. Bowing to Hyakujo, he said, "I am now emancipated from my fox existence, but allow me to ask one more favor of you. On the far side of the mountain you will find a fox's body beside a rock. Please give it a monk's funeral."

Master Hyakujo ordered the ino to strike the gong and announce to the monks that after the midday meal a funeral for a monk would be held. The monks were puzzled. None of them were sick and no monk was in the Nirvana Hall. What was this all about?

After the meal, Hyakujo led the monks to a rock on the far side of the mountain. With his staff he uncovered the body of a dead fox and had it cremated.

That evening, Hyakujo had all the monks assemble in the main hall and told them the story of the old man. When he had finished, Obaku asked,

53

"Because the old man had not given the correct turning words he was reborn five hundred times as a fox. If however he had given the correct turning words, what would have happened to him?"

Hyakujo said, "Come over here and I will tell you."

Obaku came forward and slapped Hyakujo. The Master laughed out loud, clapped his hands and said, "I thought that the foreigner's beard was red, but now I see a foreigner with a red beard."

The Teisho:

It is already the third day of sesshin and the zendo atmosphere is very good—stillness and serenity surround us. One of the most attractive parts of sesshin is the creation of such stillness. Especially right after everybody has entered the zendo, there is just the rustling sound of people preparing themselves for zazen. At one point the noise stops completely. Sh-h-h . . . no sound . . . nothing . . . When no one is in the zendo there is quiet. But that quiet and the quiet of zazen are different. Their thickness is different.

So today's koan is about that famous Hyakujo's fox. Now, as a story, this koan is very strange. It doesn't make sense. Almost every Zen koan is like that. Are koans really so nonsensical? From the ordinary point of view, yes, they are. But if we enter into a certain condition of zazen and try to comprehend them not by our brains but through our samadhi, *everything* makes great sense, in fact true sense. I will give you one or two examples.

One koan goes like this: "Without moving, stop the fight across the river!" Evidently two people are fighting on one bank of the river while you are supposed to be on the other bank of the river. "Without moving" means without going to the other side. When we hear such things, at first we get the impression that we are about to learn some magic, some special technique to solve problems.

Another koan says: "Silence that gong which is ringing from the distant mountain temple!" Sounds almost impossible! Or: "There is a stone in the bottom of the sea. Pick it up without getting your robes wet!" Impossible! Now these koans are not asking us to learn some miraculous powers. They are indirectly teaching us about One Mind or Oneness by using metaphors like "the other side of the river," "the distant mountain temple" and "the bottom of the sea." Thinking in the ordinary way, these koans are impossible to solve. But they do teach us how to become One: to become One with the fighting; to become One with the gong; to become One with the stone. Zazen is no other than the practice of becoming.

Now today's koan is teaching the same thing in a more complicated form. There are actually only two important points in the story. The first point is as Master Hakuin says in *The Song of Zazen*:

> *The virtues of perfection such as charity, morality,*
> *And the invocation of the Buddha's name,*
> *Confession and ascetic discipline,*
> *And many other good deeds of merit—*
> *All these return into THIS!*

What is THIS? THIS is the first point.

The second point is the matter of karma—the law of causation. These are the only two points of this long story that need be carefully considered. But as long I have introduced to you the entire story of Hyakujo's Fox, I'll do my best and try to explain it with the hope of inspiring our zazen practice.

Hyakujo Ekai Zenji (720–814), a Chinese Zen master of the T'ang Dynasty, was Baso's successor. Hyakujo is the author of the *Hyakujo Shingi*, a directive on the general policies and routines for Zen monasteries. It is the oldest existing document of its kind. Hyakujo died when he was ninety-four years old, and it is said that he worked every day of his life. The most famous story about Hyakujo goes as follows:

Hyakujo's students felt so sorry to see their old master still working in the fields that one day they hid his hoe. When he could not find it, and therefore could do no work, he stopped eating—one day, two days, three days. Finally the attendant monk asked him, "Why are you fasting?"

"I have to fast."

"Why?"

"I'm not working."

"But you are an old man."

55

"I have to work."

"Why?"

"A day of no work is a day of no eating."

With this reply, Hyakujo's disciples gave him back his hoe. Hyakujo's student who appears in today's koan is Obaku Kiun Zenji (d. 850?). His Chinese name is Huang Po and he is the author of *Transmission of Mind*. Obaku's successor was Rinzai Gigen Zenji (d. 866), the founder of the Rinzai school of Zen Buddhism.

To understand the story of Hyakujo's Fox, there is no need to go all the way back to T'ang Dynasty, China. The spirit of this story is not Chinese—it's American. It is not T'ang Dynasty—it's twentieth century.

Evidently Hyakujo's teishos were given outdoors, as was the custom of the times. And there was an old man with white hair, a long beard and wide-opened eyes, always attending the Dharma assembly, standing or sitting behind the monks. Nobody could see him except Master Hyakujo. Don't take this part too seriously. It is not so important whether he was seen or not seen, whether his hair was long or short, yellow, black or white. These things don't matter. Whenever the teishos ended, the monks would return to the zendo and the old man would disappear. It continued for a while. One day, after the monks had left, the old man remained. He asked permission of Master Hyakujo to speak with him.

Hyakujo asked, "Who are you?"

The old man replied, "I am not a human being. Long ago, in the days of Kasho Buddha, I was the head of this monastery."

He was either the chief monk or the abbot.

"One day, a monk asked me, 'Does the enlightened man fall into causation?' "

The enlightened man is completely free. But is he really free from all cause and effect or not?

"So I said," the old man continued, " 'the enlightened man does not fall into causation.' Because of this answer, I had to live as a fox for five hundred lifetimes—life after life. I couldn't become a human being—always fox, fox, fox . . . five hundred times! Now I beg you, Master Hyakujo! Please say the turning words and emancipate me from this fox existence."

Hyakujo said, "Why don't you ask me the same question that the monk asked you a long time ago?"

"Does the enlightened man fall into causation?"

"He is not deceived by causation!"

With this, the old man was immediately enlightened.

Now, this is something to think about! The fact that on September 5, 1976, forty-four of us gathered here for the Opening Kessei Sesshin was not an accidental happening. Every one of us has good karma and bad karma. But, as a matter of fact, it is incorrect to say that we *have* karma in the same way that we say, "I have two arms." Each one of us is karma itself. One karma is female, another karma is male—each according to various conditions. THIS is karma—condensed karma. Karma literally means "action." When we think—that is the action of the brain. When we speak—that is the action of the tongue. When we move—that is the action of the body. Every single moment we are either thinking, talking or moving. We are continually adding more karma to ourselves.

Not realizing that we are karma itself, we bumpkins think that karma is some force outside of ourselves and that we are lucky to possess it or we are lucky not to possess it. Actually, we are karma itself. It is not given to us, neither is it made by someone else. Most of us think that we have both so-called good karma and so-called bad karma. And naturally we prefer good karma. We want more good karma than bad karma and that is why people do some kind of practice. In our case, we are doing zazen practice, sitting and walking. Hakuin said, "Even those who have practiced it for just one sitting will see all their evil karma erased!"

In regard to this statement, do not think that just because you may have sat many times all of your karma has been completely washed away. Remember that, even now, at this moment, we are adding more karma. Therefore we have to continue to do this washing for as long as we live. Every morning we chant:

All the evil karma ever committed by me since of old
On account of my beginningless greed, anger and folly,

Born of my body, mouth and thought—
I now confess and purify them all.

It doesn't matter whether we call this verse "repentance," "purification" or "confession." These are just different names for the same thing. The important thing is that we should realize the fundamental necessity of doing something like "confession" or "purification." This is sound practice.

Ideas such as "enlightenment" or "freedom" may sound very attractive. But true freedom must be freedom from the deception of karma. And real emancipation must be emancipation from the deception of karma. So one of the important things in zazen practice is purification. Torei Enji Zenji (1721–1792), one of the founders of Ryutaku Monastery, emphasized the purification practice of bowing. He said that when we do zazen our bodies may be still, our tongues may be speechless, but our brains are still able to think about many things.

At first when we bow on the floor, we are filled with doubts. "What am I doing?" "How come I have to do this bowing so many times?" But the more you bow, the more you are able to feel reverence. This reverential bowing movement is as wonderful as zazen. Bowing purification, as silent, as speechless as zazen, cultivates humility and reverence. So, according to Master Torei, the best practice for growing spiritually is bowing. I once saw a Korean Zen master bowing in a zendo. Later I asked him how many times does he bow each day. He told me that every day, as a morning service, he bows one hundred and eight times. So bowing on the floor one hundred and eight times is just as good as morning service. Of course zazen is just as good as, even better than anything else. But chanting and bowing help us to erase this deception of karma. On top of all this, the zendo itself is like a huge bathtub and we are bathing in the pure air. So just to be in the zendo is itself purification.

So, "does the enlightened man fall into causation" or "has the enlightened man transcended cause and effect?" Hyakujo said, "He is not deceived by causation." Hearing this, the old man was immediately emancipated. He was no longer a fox.

Once my teacher, Soen Roshi, said, "This cause-and-effect matter is not particularly a specialty of Buddhism." Even if a man called Siddhartha Gautama or Shakyamuni Buddha had not appeared in this world, and even if there were no such teaching as Buddhism, the law of causation would still exist. No one can be free from it. No one can ignore it. But many people are deceived by it.

To speak of such things as "causation," "karma," and "deception" or to call something "repentance," "confession," or "purification" doesn't really matter. If one knows what he is doing and if one feels what he is doing, whether he is a Buddhist or not, whatever he does is perfectly all right. So let us not be bound by traditional expressions. What is important is not the word, but the spirit.

Before I resume the fox story, let me speak about a few other matters. As everybody has experienced, by the middle day of the sesshin our consciousness has either been expanded or has entered into a slightly different dimension. Through this altered consciousness we can see and hear things more clearly, as they are. Therefore, these teishos can be delivered by me and, in turn, can be comprehended by you. If this were a classroom and we were without sufficient zazen preparation, it would be difficult to communicate in a deep sense. So teisho is no longer coming from my tongue into your ears. Rather, it is hara to hara communication.

Almost all of us have been working on Mu. As this is another name for our Original Nature, no matter how many years we practice Mu, there is no end to it. All of the Zen koans, whether they are recorded in Zen texts or not, are manifestations of Mu—manifestations of our True Mind.

For those who are doing Mu, it may seem that talking about another koan, such as the fox story, is distracting. But when we consider Mu as a fundamental practice and koan work as manifestation research, there are no conflicts. So, when it comes time to do zazen, sit down, exhale completely, regulate your breath and begin repeating Mu, Mu, Mu-u-u . . . ! After a while start to chew the koan, using your total body and mind. Again, again and again! At one point, the koan integrates or penetrates into yourself. It becomes like your own flesh and blood. When the so-called answer comes out during the sitting, put it aside and go back to Mu. When it comes time to go to dokusan, bring that so-called answer. If it is rejected, forget about it. Just continue to repeat the same thing again and again until a new dimension opens.

It is prohibited for students to speak about koans to each other, even if they be husband and wife. The simple reason for this prohibition is that if a student is told how to respond to a koan, even if the teacher passes him, that knowledge is quickly forgotten. Our bodies should be completely integrated with the koan until it becomes like our own flesh and blood. So do not talk about your koan! Make it your own! A saying goes: "Even if the master says that it is all right, unless you truly feel that it is all right, do not accept his acknowledgment." Passing a koan is not like accumulating credits in school. "Oh, I got twenty-five credits" or "I got seventeen hundred credits." So what? Even one credit is enough if your koan has really become like your own flesh and blood.

Some of us have been sitting with Mu for a relatively long time and may be feeling discouraged. So I will tell you a wonderful story about Mu. My ordination teacher has a Dharma brother-monk named Soho Matsuura, who stayed in a monastery for thirteen years, with no discontinuation. Thirteen years straight! And for thirteen years he worked on Mu. On the day that he arrived at the monastery as a new monk, Mu was assigned to him and through innumerable sesshins and, indeed, through innumerable dokusans, he continued Mu. One day during teisho, the roshi of that monastery said to everybody (that monk's Buddhist name being Soho, he was called Ho-san in the monastery), "Well, some of you new monks have testified a little bit to what Mu really is. Congratulations!" There is very subtle sarcasm here. The roshi continued, "But Ho-san's Mu is really *something*! Though he hasn't yet passed it, it is so deeply penetrated that he can no longer pass. It has become one Mu."

The years passed and Ho-san became an abbot of a temple in Tokyo. When I first met him he was nearly sixty years old. I visited his temple and found him sweeping the leaves off the moss with a bamboo broom. He was working in the temple cemetery. When I saw his cleaning style it all fit so well. There was no extra space between Ho-san, the broom, the moss, the leaves and the entire cemetery. No superfluous action! Just with it! I was so impressed. Later when I heard the "thirteen years

Mu" story, I thought to myself, "No wonder!" I am telling you about Ho-san because some of you may be worrying about not passing Mu. But Mu is not something to pass. You must make it your own flesh and blood. Naturally this takes time. Even if it takes your whole lifetime, that's perfectly all right.

The more we sit, the less we are disturbed by conditions, good or bad. "Today I am so high" or "This afternoon I became so low, I wonder why." So on and so forth. The more we sit the more we can transcend so-called good and bad, liking and disliking. To make such preferences is a disease of the mind. What we are searching for is to be little by little freed from such preferences. So I tell you, don't rush! But also I tell you, be diligent!

Now many things happen during sesshin and pain is the most difficult problem. There are many methods for overcoming pain: this exercise or that mental attitude, etc. But nothing works all the time, except perseverance. Perseverance not only reduces the degree of pain but, by itself, it is a wonderful practice for perfecting the virtue of endurance.

Be with it! Be with it!

Someone once said to me:

> A fly brushes my eye,
> And the pain vanishes.
> Mu-u-u-u!

This is a wonderful haiku. With no intention of composing poetry, this person just spoke factuality as factuality. So at one point the pain does vanish.

Getting back to the fox story . . . that evening, after the fox's body had been cremated, Hyakujo had all the monks assemble in the zendo and told them the story of the old man. When he had finished Obaku asked, "Because the old man had not given the correct turning words he was reborn five hundred times as a fox. If however he had given the correct turning words, what would have happened to him?"

As the chief monk of Hyakujo's monastery, Obaku already had clear understanding. By asking about the old man, he was attempting to engage his teacher in Dharma battle. "If however the old man's answer had been correct, each time that he was born he would have progressed from fox to human being, from human being to Bodhisattva, from Bodhisattva to Buddha. Then from Buddha to what?!"

Hyakujo said, "Come over here. I will tell you."

Obaku then stepped toward Hyakujo and slapped him.

There was a master in China and whenever he was asked, "What is the Ultimate Truth?" he would strike the earth and make a loud noise. POW!

What is Zen Buddhism?

POW!

What is Buddha?

POW!

This Zen master was called Tachi Osho because of this POW! *Ta* means "to strike" and *chi* means "earth"—The Master of Earth-Striking. The more we sit, the more we condense ourselves. Condense! Condense! Condense! Just-Mu is the final condensation. Now, what is the difference between Tachi's POW!, Obaku's slap! and Master Hakuin's THIS? Obaku certainly knew this matter. He knew that all Hyakujo could do, all that he could say, all that he could give is this slap. Therefore Obaku simply took the initiative. This is the part that is most often misunderstood. Why did the disciple strike the teacher's face? He didn't especially have to strike his face, any place would have been enough. POW! This is enough. But, besides sitting, besides entering deep samadhi, Zen requires spirit—vital, dynamic spirit. It is not only a matter of being quiet—that's not what Zen is. POW! POW! Each time, POW! Even striking the hand and sounding the clappers in the zendo are no other than THIS! Just at the right moment, not too soon, not too late—strike! POW! POW! Strike with intensity! Then, with this sound, someone may realize THIS.

In order to express the dynamic dynamism, with dynamic action, Obaku struck Hyakujo. Hyakujo already knew that his beloved student possessed a degree of spirituality as profound as his own. So as an acknowledgment, he said, "I thought that the foreigner's beard was red, but now I see a foreigner with a red beard."

Now let me read Mumon's comment:

Not falling into causation, why was he turned into a fox? Not being deceived by causation, why was he emancipated from the fox's body. If you have an enlightened eye and can see through THIS, then you will know that the old man did enjoy his five hundred happy, blessed lives as a fox.

To end this teisho I should like to point out THIS matter: if you understand THIS matter whether you say that an enlightened man does not fall into causation or an enlightened man is not deceived by causation doesn't matter. On the other hand, if you do not understand THIS matter, no matter what lofty, poetic expressions you may use, they will never be enough. Now, let me ask you: "Does the enlightened man fall into causation?"

Dai Bosatsu Zendo Kongo-ji
September 7 and 8, 1976

Joshu's Perfect Way

The Blue Rock Collection: Case 2

Introductory Words:

If you stabilize your faith and realize the Perfect Way, you cannot help but feel that heaven and earth are not big, but small. You will see the sun, moon and stars lose their light and become like black beans. Even all the Buddhas, Bodhisattvas and all the patriarchs in the past, present and future have to go through the practice in order to know this matter. No sutra contains a single complete phrase which expresses the Perfect Way as it is. No teacher can speak about the Perfect Way completely. In fact, if you say "Buddha" or "Zen," you have to wash out your mouth with soap. Then, how can a newcomer learn this matter, and how can an old-timer teach this matter? Here is a case.

Look!

The Koan:

Attention!

A Chinese Zen master, Joshu, once gave a lecture to his disciples. He said, "The Perfect Way is not difficult. As it is, it goes beyond all preferences.

"When you speak, your words are either confused or clear. Look at me! I remain neither in confusion nor clarity. How about you?"

Thus the lecture ended.

A monk stood up and asked, "If you remain neither in the state of confusion nor clarity, where are you?"

Joshu replied, "I don't know."

The monk continued, "If you don't know, then how can you speak about it?"

Joshu said, "This interview is finished. You had better bow and retire."

The Teisho:

The Dharma takes care of those who do zazen.

This is the middle day of sesshin. The zendo atmosphere is getting more and more lucid and our actions are becoming less and less awkward. This is not a matter of reason, but a matter of actuality. So to act according to sesshin discipline and to spend seven days living and sitting with other people—these themselves are wonderful practices. Tomorrow will be even better.

Speaking about better and worse, let us once again understand a very simple fact—that nothing is permanent. No zazen condition is permanent, no profound samadhi lasts forever and no miserable zazen lasts forever. It is because of long, long years of habit that we prefer good and dislike bad; that we pass judgments and give comments. So, practice, practice, practice! Practice implies constant effort. We know how useless it is to judge our own zazen. "I had hoped that this afternoon would be better, but unexpectedly something happened and now my zazen is miserable." This kind of thinking is just a waste of time. So, let us practice to be less judgmental, more single-minded. And with this single-mindedness, become fools.

Ever since we were born, we have been practicing to become more clever and more wise. But we have never practiced to become fools. Now our wisdom, little by little, teaches us, especially when we are in quiet contemplation, that mere cleverness and wiseness produce lots of problems. But we are terribly afraid of becoming fools. We are as fearful of becoming fools as we are of dying. Master Hakuin said:

My dear beloved students, die once while you are still alive.
Then you can truly live and you will never die again.

To die in this sense means no other than to become a fool. To be a fool means doing Mu, just Mu after Mu, without adding your commentaries, compliments, analysis, criticisms and/or doubts. Mu! Mu! Mu! Mu like a fool. This is what our practice is and this is the most effective practice. This is what Hakuin calls "die"! So let us not be afraid of becoming fools. We do not lose our cleverness and our wisdom when we become fools while doing zazen. In fact, we become even more clever and more wise. The essence of Zen is so simple that it can be described in one short word—*JUST*. Just! Just this! This right here, right now . . . Mu! Put up no resentment, no resistance, for these are impediments to our practice. In Japanese monasteries there is a strict system of seniority. No monk may change the order of things. No one says, "I believe this is best" or "I think that . . ." or "In my opinion . . . ." So let us become fools who can accept this *as it is-ness*. Practice without ceasing!

Today's koan is the second case of the *Hekigan Roku, The Blue Rock Collection*. Engo's introductory words go like this:

> *If you stabilize your faith and realize the Perfect Way, you cannot help but feel that heaven and earth are not big, but small.*

"If you stabilize your faith. . . ." Faith. . . . There is a wonderful quotation from the *Rinzai Roku*, the sayings of Master Rinzai, translated by D. T. Suzuki:

> *Do you know where the disease lies which keeps you learners from reaching true understanding? It lies where you have no faith in yourself. When faith in yourself is lacking you find yourselves hurried by others in every possible way. At every encounter you are no longer your master; you are driven about by others, this way and that.*
>
> *All that is required is all at once to cease leaving yourself in search of something external. When this is done you will find yourself no different from the Buddhas or patriarchs.*

Faith is necessary in zazen practice. Uncertainty discourages us. Certainty leaves us free to march on. Have faith in your zazen.

What is faith? In the case of shikantaza, faith is to believe that cause and effect are occurring simultaneously. One minute of sitting in shikantaza is one minute of revelation of Buddha nature. In the case of daily zazen, faith is to believe that cause appears at one time and effect will occur sooner or later. So daily sitting is an accumulation of our own efforts, and when the time is ready, we will all reach true understanding, that is, the understanding that even while we were "reaching," we had actually already "reached." Accumulation expedites the readiness. With this belief we can do zazen. So stabilize your faith firmly and realize this matter!

Once someone asked Hakuun Yasutani Roshi, "What is the best way to become enlightened?"

He replied, "The very moment you can believe in what you are doing one hundred per cent is the very moment you will become enlightened."

With no expectation of some miraculous visitation, with no reluctance, and certainly with no resistance, we sit. A fool has little sense of judgment. A fool has few words and few emotional reactions. This kind of "fool practice," in fact, made this Dai Bosatsu Zendo possible. One retarded boy's chanting of Shu jo mu hen sei gan do became an indispensable element towards the establishment of this zendo:

> *However innumerable all beings are, I vow to enlighten them all.*

Let me quote a passage to you from the book *Namu Dai Bosa*, which explains about this matter:

"I want now to mention one extremely important step on the Way to Dai Bosatsu. Without it, this story would be like a mandala with no center.

Earlier I mentioned the name of Mrs. Shubin Tanahashi. A student of Nyogen Senzaki, it was she who discovered Soen Roshi's poem in the Japanese magazine, *Fujin Koron*, and showed it to her teacher (Nyogen Senzaki). With her discovery the mysterious karmic drama started. How then was it that Mrs. Tanahashi and Nyogen Senzaki met, and how was it that she became his student?

Thus have I heard:

Shubin is her Dharma name; her real name is Kin Sago. She was born in Gifu Prefecture in Japan in 1897 and came to America as an immigrant when she was eighteen years old. She married Mr. Tanahashi and together they ran a laundry shop in downtown Los

Angeles. They had four children. The last child was born in 1920; he was a boy named Sumio, but people called him Jimmy.

Jimmy was a seriously retarded child. Mrs. Tanahashi's sorrow and her devotion to this unfortunate son affected her life tremendously. He needed far more attention and care than an ordinary child—almost more than she could give him. As a result, her life became busier and busier, the burden heavier and heavier, both family and business affairs keeping her constantly at work. In the spring of 1932, when she was thirty-five years old, an exotic-looking Japanese priest brought a bundle of dirty clothes to her laundry shop. A few weeks passed, but he did not return to claim his laundry. So one day, Mrs. Tanahashi delivered his laundry to him at his apartment. At that time he said to her, "Thank you. I am sorry I did not come to pick up my laundry, but I did not have enough money."

During this first enounter Mrs. Tanahashi learned that the man's name was Nyogen Senzaki and that he was a Zen Buddhist monk. He had just moved from San Francisco to Los Angeles and had started a small Zen group there. Although Mrs. Tanahashi did not know anything about Zen Buddhism, she knew she was in need of some spiritual support.

At that first meeting Nyogen Senzaki asked Mrs. Tanahashi if she was interested in writing waka poetry. If so, he said that he would be happy to help her polish her work. Gradually the two of them began to know each other. Then one day she mentioned Jimmy and described her situation. Nyogen Senzaki said to her, "All right, I will take care of Jimmy for you, two or three hours a day. I will baby-sit with him."

The following day, she recalls, he came to the shop and took Jimmy in the stroller. Although Jimmy was already twelve years old, he needed to be pushed in a stroller, for he was unable to get around by himself. After that Nyogen Senzaki came every day to her shop and spent two or three hours with Jimmy. While walking along the streets of downtown Los Angeles with the boy, Nyogen Senzaki would chant, *Shu jo mu hen sei gan do* ("However innumerable all beings are, I vow to enlighten them all"), again and again, innumerable times. Although the retarded boy was unable to speak, he eventually was able to utter these syllables.

The baby-sitting helped Mrs. Tanahashi. Perhaps Nyogen Senzaki was also able to have his laundry done free of charge. However, the real significance of this encounter lies in a realm much deeper than that of mere exchange of labor.

One day Nyogen Senzaki said to Mrs. Tanahashi, "Recently I have been wondering if I should do some Dharma work in America with Jimmy." In the fall of that year—oddly enough, just around the time of my birth—she became his student. By the time she found the poem in the *Fujin Koron* in 1934, their teacher-student relationship was well established.

Years passed and it became necessary to send Jimmy to an institution in California called the Pacific Colony, where many people with similar handicaps lived under the care of the State of California.

One summer afternoon when I was in Los Angeles with Shubin Tanahashi, she said, "Today I am going to visit Jimmy. Would you like to come?"

"Yes, I would," I answered.

By that time I knew all about Jimmy and the mysterious Dharma relations somehow clustering around his illness; Shubin-san's encounter with Nyogen Senzaki; Nyogen Senzaki's discovery of Soen Nakagawa; Soen Roshi's journey to America; and through Soen Roshi, my coming to America.

We took a bus and went to the Pacific Colony. It was a hot California summer afternoon. I was naturally wearing a black monk's robe. Jimmy, who was then about forty years old, had never seen me before. But the moment he saw me or, more precisely, the moment he saw someone wearing a black Buddhist monk's robe— he struggled to put his palms together in gassho, but he was unable to bring his two hands together evenly. The fingers of one hand curled around the tips of the other; spittle drooled from his lips as he attempted to drag out words from a mouth which could not articulate without great effort. At last, very slowly and almost unrecognizably, came the syllables *Shu jo mu hen sei gan do* . . .

I had never been so affected by any chanting in my life. On August 28, 1966, Jimmy Tanahashi passed away. He was forty-six years old. However, his Bodhisattva spirit has not departed. *Shu jo mu hen sei gan do*, "However innumerable all beings are, I vow to enlighten them all."

The birth of International Dai Bosatsu Zendo Kongo-ji is a perfect example of karmic drama. The Dai Bosatsu Mandala, along with all the many known and unknown actors and actresses who have figured prominently in its intricate and unimaginable design, is now taking form. The name of the drama is *Namu Dai Bosa*. Karma is the producer; Dharma, the director; and all beings are the cast.

At the time of this writing, just one year before the official opening, the construction of International Dai Bosatsu Zendo has almost been completed. The new monastery stands amidst emerald-green forests at the edge of Beecher Lake, waiting to receive travelers from all directions.

I have been walking on the Way to Dai Bosatsu for many years. When did this pilgrimage really begin? Was it when I left Japan in 1960? Or was it when I went to Rvutaku-ji for the first time? Or was it when I learned the *Heart Sutra* at the age of nine? None of these seems quite right. And yet I am unable to say that it started at the time I was born, or that it had been arranged in my previous life. Perhaps the best, in fact the only, way to say it is that from the beginningless beginning I have been walking toward this goal.

Now, seeing Dai Bosatsu Zendo appearing tangibly in front of me, this goal seems still far away—farther than ever. This comes as a surprise at first—but at the next moment, I realize that this is as it should be. The Way to Dai Bosatsu has no end. I am walking on this Way toward an endless end, and I cannot but continue."

So sometimes a fool is wiser than a clever person. So become a fool! And like Jimmy, have a vow! In this particular lifetime, besides some personal goals, everybody, I believe, should have a vow, one that is unselfish; one that is made with no expectations of return benefits.

This is a Bodhisattva vow and with it anybody, even a fool, can become a walking Bodhisattva. This makes life more meaningful. Fool! Become a fool with a Bodhisattva Vow and a lucid mind. Lucid Mind! Do fool's zazen, no judgments, no calculations, no returns. Just! Just! Just! And once again, JUST!

Now, getting back to Engo's introductory words: "If you stabilize your faith you will realize the Perfect Way."

Zazen as we are doing now, whether we sit in full lotus, half-lotus, quarter-lotus, *seiza* (Japanese style) or on a chair, is not a religion as such. This is a practice of humanity. Through zazen you can realize the Perfect Way.

Let me speak about the matter of *shusho* and *honbun*: existential and fundamental. Existentially speaking there is no Perfect Way; something is always wrong. But fundamentally speaking, there is no way which is not perfect. We human beings are so familiar with the existential understanding of life that we think that we can find something which is perfect, and so we are constantly seeking. As Master Hakuin says:

We are like the son of a rich man
Who wandered away among the poor.

We seek something, somewhere outside. We do not realize that this fundamental Perfect Way and this existential imperfect way exist simultaneously. The Perfect Way is neither hidden nor is it located in a particular place. Zazen practice is no other than the realization of "this matter."

"This matter" has many labels—according to the Christians it is God; according to the Chinese philosophers it is Tao; according to Joshu it is Mu; according to Soen Roshi it is Endless Dimension Universal Life. But it is not a matter to be discovered. It is simply a matter of realization. In fact, by now, after sitting many hours in sesshin, some people tell me that the differentiation between subjectivity and objectivity has become less and less. They feel more and more "one." Or they tell me that for the first time they understand the meaning of One Mind. Everything we do here is related, leading us to "this matter." When you believe this, this belief itself stabilizes your way.

The introductory words continue: "If you understand this, you cannot help but feel that heaven and earth (the whole universe or cosmos) are really small, not big." In general we think that the universe is vast. We think that the universe contains innumerable stars. But the moment we define the universe as vast, containing innumerable stars, that is the very moment that we limit the limitless universe. As it is said in the *Diamond Sutra*: "What is called the 'world' is not the world, therefore we call it world." A more comprehensible example of this kind of rationale is shikantaza. There is no such practice as shikantaza, therefore we call it shikantaza. The moment we define our practice as shikantaza is the very moment we limit the span of shikantaza. Shikantaza is the practice which we somehow go into, by breath-counting, through Mu or, for some people, through chanting. You go into the state where you no longer Mu, no longer count, no longer chant. And the mind is as lucid as it possibly can be. The hara is as firm as it possibly can be. So shikantaza is a condition which we go into and it is not the practice which we do. You cannot really say, "I am doing the practice of shikantaza." Instead, more properly, we should say, "JUST SITTING." The difference is so subtle. "A tenth of an inch's difference and heaven and earth are set apart." If this tiny subtlety is understood, it makes the difference between heaven and earth.

The introductory words continue with this typical Zen expression: "You will see the sun, moon and stars lose their light and become like black beans." This means that through your own realization, your light becomes even brighter than the sun, moon and stars. An interesting part of Zen Buddhism is learning to interpret this kind of Chinese imagery. To say that when you become enlightened you become brighter, illuminating the whole universe, is not bad. To say that the sun, the moon and the stars lose their light and become like black beans may confuse you, but this statement has more impact.

Next: "Even all the Buddhas, Bodhisattvas and patriarchs have to go through this stabilization of faith and realization of the Perfect Way"—with pain. There is a Japanese proverb which goes: "He who buys cheaply, spends more." If you buy something cheap it will break soon and you will have to buy another one. Easy training doesn't help.

Nectar-sweet words are of no use. Another proverb goes: "Good medicine is always bitter." Good advice is always difficult to accept and good practice may be excruciatingly painful. This pain is an indispensable part of our valuable practice. After doing zazen for over twenty-five years I still have pain. I often think that if there were no pain, the taste of zazen would become dull. Zazen with no pain is like eating noodles without sesame seeds and other condiments. The taste of the noodles alone is bland. Even the patriarchs had to pass through.

Now the patriarchs are always talking about "this matter." But what exactly is it? Wherever we are and whatever we are doing, the existential phenomena, such as pain and joy, and the unchangeable, eternal reality are always revealing themselves simultaneously. To realize this fact is called "this matter" of Mu. . . . No *sutra* contains a single complete phrase which expresses the Perfect Way as it is. No teacher can speak about the Perfect Way completely. Yet every single individual, including the woodchuck eating the grasses during kinhin, the birds singing, the sounds of the cool breeze, the innumerable stars in the sky, the uncountable fireflies in the meadow—all are revealing the Perfect Way, completely, as it is. According to Master Hakuin:

> *At this moment, what more need we seek?*
> *As the Truth eternally reveals itself,*
> *This very place is the Lotus Land of Purity,*
> *This very body is the Body of the Buddha*

To say that something is wonderful is as bad as saying "Buddha" or "Zen" or "realization" or "existential reality" or "fundamental reality." "You have to wash your mouth out with soap." And yet to shut up is as bad as to say something. This is indeed a dilemma.

Now we approach the main koan: "Joshu's Perfect Way."

Since some of you are perhaps not familiar with Joshu Jushin Zenji (778–897), let me briefly introduce this outstanding Zen master of the T'ang Dynasty. When he was eighteen, it is said that he had an experience called *hakasantaku*. This is a marvelous Chinese expression. *Ha* means "break"; *ka* means "house"; *san* means "scattered" or "spread"; *taku* is a building. This "broken house" or "scattered building" refers to the *alaya* consciousness, the storehouse of all our experiences and memories. So metaphorically speaking, hakasantaku means to break the house, to scatter all the pieces of furniture. Everything disappears. So Joshu's preconceived notions dropped away at the age of eighteen. With this freedom of life, Joshu visited Master Nansen. It was a summer afternoon and Nansen was taking a nap. Nansen asked the young boy, who later became Joshu, "Where are you from?"

Joshu answered, "I am from the temple of Jizo." Joshu's temple must have been named after a statue of Jizo Bodhisattva.

Nansen while still lying down asked again, "Oh, I see. So I assume that you have had enough time to bow to Jizo Bodhisattva?"

Joshu then bowed to Nansen. With this dynamic, spontaneous action, Nansen thought, "Oh, this is not an ordinary boy." He asked, "Do you have a teacher?"

Again Joshu bowed to Nansen and said, "How do you do, my teacher?" Thus Joshu became Nansen's disciple.

Joshu continued to study and practice until the age of sixty. From eighteen to sixty is forty-two years! From sixty to eighty he spent his time mostly going on pilgrimages, visiting Zen masters. There is a famous dialogue concerning Joshu and Rinzai. When Rinzai was washing his feet, Joshu came along and asked, "Why did Bodhidharma come from India to China?" (What is the essence of Buddha-Dharma?)

Rinzai answered, "Right now, I am washing my feet."

Joshu came closer, acting as if he had not heard what Rinzai had said. It goes without saying that what Rinzai said to Joshu and the manner in which Joshu responded are no other than the very essence of Buddha-Dharma.

Master Rinzai said, "If you pretend not to understand, now I have to pour out the dirty water."

Then Joshu departed.

So Joshu continued his pilgrimages until the age of eighty. Normally, the age of sixty is the time to retire and the age of eighty is the time to die. But Joshu began his teaching career at the age of eighty and continued until he was one hundred and twenty.

A monk asked Joshu, "Has a dog Buddha nature or not?"

Joshu replied, with his matured, well-polished, well-cultivated, well-trained and well-enlightened tongue, "MU!"

And ever since, not only in China, but all over Japan and now almost all over America, Zen students are saying Mu, Mu, Mu! Mu is so effective that because of it innumerable people have had their lives changed from bad to good, from worse to better.

Now, at last, the main koan: "The Perfect Way is not difficult. As it is, it goes beyond all preferences."

Actually, Joshu was quoting the opening lines of *Believing in Mind* by the Third Patriarch, Sosan Ganchi Zenji. The expression "Perfect Way" impresses us as if all things around us are imperfect while there is something which is perfect somewhere else. This is not true. To sit, to walk and even to trip and fall down are no other than the Perfect Way itself. To be silent, to laugh and even to scream are the Perfect Way. Everyday action is the Perfect Way. If this is understood there is no more worry about your not being perfect. So we have to change our definition of perfection. If we seek so-called "perfection," we will never get it. Perfect peace on earth will never, never come. Nonetheless, at this moment, at this place, we do feel peaceful—chanting, sitting, eating, breathing, Mu-ing—each action is perfect as it is and cannot be otherwise! It is unnecessary to name them "difficult" or "easy."

"When you speak, your words are either confused or clear. Look at me! I remain neither in confusion nor clarity. How about you?"

Thus the lecture ended.

A monk stood up and asked Joshu, "If you remain in neither the state of confusion nor clarity, where are you?"

Joshu replied, "I don't know."

"I don't know"—this "I don't know," is it the same as Bodhidharma's "I don't know" or Emperor Wu's "I don't know"? Don't answer me, "I don't know."

When the unenlightened monk attempted to attack Joshu with logic, saying, "If you don't know, how can you speak about such matters," transcending logic and showing the Perfect Way as it is, Joshu said,

"This interview is finished. You had better bow and retire."

Thus my teisho is over. With no difficulties, transcending all preferences, we should all return to the zendo and continue our zazen.

Dai Bosatsu Zendo Kongo-ji
July 2 and 3, 1975

Not Wind, Not Flag

The Gateless Gate: Case 29

The Koan:

A temple flag was flapping in the wind. Two monks were arguing about it. One said that the flag was moving. The other one said that the wind was moving. Arguing back and forth, they could come to no agreement.

The Sixth Patriarch said, "It is neither the wind nor the flag. But it is your minds that are moving."

The two monks were astonished.

The Verse:

> *The wind moves, the flag moves,*
> *The mind moves.*
> *All of them missed it.*
> *Though he knows how to open his mouth,*
> *He does not see that he was caught with*
>   *words.*

The Teisho:

Today's story is quite interesting. It is the story of the Sixth Patriarch, Eno Daikan Zenji Dai Osho (638–713). The honorific titles *Zenji Dai Osho* mean "Zen Master and Venerable Teacher." Eno was unquestionably one of the most important teachers in the history of Zen Buddhism in China.

The first important matter to talk about is Eno's definition of zazen. We modern people are quite accustomed to defining things. We are always asking, "What does this mean?" And we are always supposed to be ready to answer, "This means such and such." Using Eno's *The Platform Scripture of the Sixth Patriarch*, I shall describe his definition of zazen. But first I will give you a literal translation. The *za* part of zazen means "sitting" and the *zen* part is usually translated as "meditation." Keep this in your mind. What then is meant by "sitting in meditation" as the Sixth Patriarch defines it?

To sit means to be free from all obstacles, not allowing thoughts to arise in the mind.

There are lots of obstacles around us, but "to be free from obstacles" means not to fight them, not to hate them. This is to be free—to transcend. Be free from all obstacles and do not allow thoughts to arise in the mind.

To meditate means to realize one's original nature and to see the imperturbability of Mind.

This is rather abstract, so I will give you a concrete metaphor. We are living on this earth. On the earth there is constantly changing weather: beautiful days, snowy days, cloudy days, rainy days. On the earth, too, are the oceans. Constantly changing waves are being formed, some high, some low. Human beings who inhabit the earth are being born and passing away—some even at this moment. Changing weather, changing oceans, changing human beings! And yet this earth itself exists as if nothing is happening. Imperturbability!

To meditate means to realize the imperturbability of one's original nature. This is the definition of zazen by Eno Daikan Zenji, the Sixth Patriarch.

After Eno received the successorship, the Fifth Patriarch told him, "You should hide yourself some place in the mountains and do more sitting practice, inconspicuously."

This is traditionally important. Many Zen masters in the past spent years of inconspicuous practice before starting to teach. It is said that Eno Daikan Zenji spent over ten years in the mountains. The day that he came down from the mountains is the very day that today's story took place.

According to tradition, each temple had a preaching sign or flag. You may remember another koan which goes:

> *Ananda asked Mahakashyapa, "I understand that the Buddha gave you a golden robe and a bowl as symbols of successorship. Did he give you anything else?"*
> *Mahakashyapa called, "Ananda!"*
> *Ananda answered, "Yes?"*
> *"Knock down the preaching sign at the gate!"*

Like this story, there must have been a preaching flag in front of the gate of the temple. This temple, by the way, was called Hosho-ji. *Ho* means "Dharma," *sho* means "nature" and *ji* is "temple," so, Dharma Nature Temple. At Hosho-ji two monks were arguing; one claiming that the wind was moving, the other one insisting that the flag was moving. Arguing in such a manner, back and forth, they could reach no agreement. Watching these monks, Eno decided to end their arguing. "It is not the wind, not the flag. It is your minds that are moving."

Hearing this, the two monks were very much surprised. They very respectfully invited Eno into the temple.

When the wind moves, the flag moves. When there is no wind, the flag does not move. If there is a wind, but no flag, no flag moves. The implication of this argument is that there is something which is called the subject and there is something which is called the object. There is something which is called human being and there is something which is called environment. Quite frequently we are very much influenced by our surroundings and by the people around us. Somehow, most of us are not yet completely free to control our own environment or circumstances. Sometimes we receive negative influences. Sometimes we receive positive influences. Zazen practice is like what Master Rinzai said:

> *If you become the master of each circumstance, wherever you stand, whatever you do, that is the Truth itself!*

Zazen practice is certainly not going into a trance or becoming a forgetful person. Rather, zazen practice makes us the master of each moment. More concretely, right now you are the master of the audience and I am the master of the speaker. You are not the master of one of the many who make up the audience, but you are the master of The Audience so that you should feel responsible to listen to what I am saying. Certainly, I am responsible to speak. At this very moment, under these circumstances, to become a master means that you become a good audience. It does not mean that you are free to sleep. To become master, in my case, means to talk entertainingly and inspiringly. Zazen is, after all, the Practice to become the master.

We often think that zazen is something special, alienated from ordinary life, quieting, etc. But if there is no connection between life and sitting, it is better to study something else. Zazen means to practice, to learn how to be the master of each different circumstance. More concretely, in the tea ceremony, the one who makes the tea is the host, but he is also the master of himself. Therefore he is the master-host. The one who receives the tea, the guest, is also the master—the master-guest. Sometimes, when the second bowl of tea is served, the guest turns the tray of sweets and pushes it towards the host. Guest and host instantly change. Now there is a new host and a new guest. The host knows that the guest did this purposely, but if he is not well trained, the host may complain, "What? What? I can't do it." This is not good. So when you are the guest, watch and if some opportunity arises, take it! Become the instant master!

These kinds of things are constantly happening to us. Zazen is therefore, in a sense, preparation for the many unpredictable and unexpected happenings in our lives. We must learn to accept them as they are. We must learn to act as master. This is what Master Rinzai means when he says:

If you can become the master of each circumstance, then wherever you stand, whatever you do, that is the Truth itself.

In any case, these two monks unquestionably knew the very famous Buddhist phrase: "Nothing exists outside of Mind." So the wind and the flag must be something inside of Mind. Nevertheless, they were arguing. Then the Sixth Patriarch said, "It is neither the wind, nor the flag, but your minds that are moving."

Now, we have to think, is this really so or not? Theoretically speaking, if all the things on this earth or universe are nothing but Mind, the movement of the wind is no other than the movement of Mind and the movement of the flag is the movement of Mind, too. What was happening was neither the movement of the wind, the flag, nor the mind.

When I swing my arms, you can see my sleeves waving. My sleeves are *just* waving . . . not the wind, not the flag, not the mind, not my sleeves. *Just* waving! Now this is factuality. It is a good hint for our zazen practice. Just THIS! THIS, not minds, not the Mind, not Mu, not the body, not the past, not the future, not even the present; not the Buddha, not the Dharma, not the Sangha, but Just THIS! It is not me, not others, not all sentient beings. Just THIS! But, it is not even THIS, that or it. When this is done, then THIS is being realized. We are as we are and nothing else. But when we say, "We are as we are," or when we speak about "thusness" or "suchness," we are far away from the factuality.

Now I will tell you an interesting story. During the T'ang Dynasty, the golden age of Zen, there lived a master called Tosan. Because of his virtue, he was quite well known and many pilgrims came to see him on top of the mountain where he lived. At the bottom of the mountain was a nun, living in a hut. She was a very enlightened nun and acted as a kind of gatekeeper. One autumn evening, seventeen Zen students, who had traveled all the way from the north to see Tosan, arrived at the nun's hut. Because it was too late to start climbing the mountain, they decided to stay at the gatehouse and to continue their journey on the following day. The gatehouse mistress, the elderly nun, invited them to spend the night with her. The seventeen monks took off their hats and their sandals, came in and immediately sat down. The nun offered to cook them a meal and so she retired to the kitchen. While she was cooking, the seventeen monks started to discuss the koan about the Sixth Patriarch, the wind and the flag. They were having a very concentrated argument. Although the nun was in the kitchen, she was able to overhear their talk. At one point she came out and said, "Come on you monks! What are you talking about?"

"We are talking about very important matters."

The nun did not say anything. Then they had dinner.

After dinner, before they went to bed, the nun said, "All right, let's get together once again."

They gathered together and resumed their talk about the koan: the two monks were arguing; the Sixth Patriarch appeared; one said that the wind was moving; the other one said that the flag was moving; the third one said that minds were moving. Then this enlightened woman gatehouse keeper said, "They are all wrong!"

One of the seventeen monks asked her, "Why do you say so?"

The nun replied, "It is not the wind, it is not the flag, it is not the mind. It is *just*"—and she started to wave her long sleeves.

The seventeen monks were, all at once, enlightened. On the next morning they decided that it was no longer necessary to see Tosan. So they began their journey home. Wonderful story!

Dai Bosatsu Zendo Kongo-ji
April 7, 1977

Gutei's Finger

The Gateless Gate: Case 3

The Koan:

Master Gutei raised his finger whenever he was asked a question. A young attendant monk began to imitate him. When anyone asked the young monk about his master's teachings he would raise his finger. Gutei heard about this mischief, and seized the young monk and cut off his finger. The young monk cried and started to run away, but Gutei called to him. When the monk turned his head, Gutei raised his own finger. In that instant the young monk was enlightened.

When Gutei was about to die he gathered his monks around him and said, "I attained my finger Zen from my teacher, Tenryu, and through-out my life it was never exhausted."

After saying this Gutei passed away.

The Teisho:

Today is September the 9th. The ninth day of the ninth month. January 1st, February 2nd, March 3rd, April 4th, May 5th, June 6th, July 7th, August 8th, today, October 10th, November 11th and December 12th—these are somewhat mysterious days. And today is the fifth day of our one-hundred-day kessei—ninety-five more days to go.

The days and nights are beautiful, indeed beautiful. Ideal surroundings and ideal food. Once in a while we should think about the tenzo's efforts. Since some of you are not familiar with the Japanese term "tenzo" I should like to tell you about it.

When the Buddhist tradition was first transmitted to the West, many new terms came with it. But for some of these terms no exact English equivalent could be found. The word Zen is a good example. Actually "zen" is the Japanese pronunciation of the transliterated Sanskrit word *dhyana*, usually translated as "meditation." But zen is more than mere

83

meditation. Another example of a non-translatable word is "sesshin." Yes, sesshin is a kind of seclusion, a kind of retreat, but neither "seclusion" nor "retreat" fully describes its total impact. Since we cannot find any appropriate equivalent in English, in order to insure that the exact nature of sesshin is not oversimplified, we just have to use the original Japanese. In the same way, if tenzo were translated as "cook" or "chef," its original and spiritual implications would be lost. The monastery tenzo is more than a cook, more than a chef. To illustrate this crucial point, I should like to tell you two stories from *The Teachings of Tenzo* by Dogen Zenji. When I was training in a monastery and doing tenzo, I read these stories and was very much inspired.

Young Dogen Zenji went to China to visit monasteries for practice and study. One day at one of the monasteries, on a very hot June afternoon, he saw the elderly tenzo working hard outside the kitchen. He was spreading out seaweed to dry on a straw mat. Dried seaweed keeps a long time, and therefore can be served throughout the year. While watching this elderly man, Dogen Zenji asked, "Sir, how old are you?"

"I am sixty-eight years old."

"Why don't you use an assistant for such strenuous work?"

The elderly tenzo replied, "He is not me!"

But Dogen Zenji still continued, "You are too serious. At your age you have to take care of yourself. The sun is so strong. Why don't you take it easy? Please rest."

The tenzo answered, "Rest? For how long?"

This short conversation may remind some of you of the great saying: "If not me, who?" So what the old tenzo was saying is: What I do is solely my own work. If I have someone substitute for me it is no longer my work. And the virtue of tenzo, that is, the virtue of doing difficult work in order to serve others, is no longer mine to perfect. How can I rest? If I don't work now when the sun is strong, the seaweed will not dry. "If not now, when?"

The second story concerning tenzo took place when Dogen had first arrived in China. Another elderly tenzo monk had come to the ship to buy some dried mushrooms. After conversing with the young Dogen for some time, the monk said, "I have to go back to the monastery to cook for the monks."

Dogen said, "Maybe someone will do it for you. Please stay here with me tonight so that we can talk some more."

"No, I have to be getting back."

"Why at your advanced age do you have to cook instead of doing zazen and studying the scriptures?"

Then this elderly tenzo said rather sarcastically to Dogen, "You young gaijin! ('Gaijin' is a rather rude term meaning foreigner or outsider.) You don't know what practice is!"

With these words the elderly tenzo left for his monastery.

For some of you these stories carry quite a heavy load. For others, they hold nothing special. It all depends on each person's degree of practice.

The tenzo, therefore, is one of the officers of the monastery whose main function is to prepare the food for the monks. But if that were all he had to do, then any kind of cook would suffice. The difference between a cook and a tenzo is that the tenzo works in the kitchen as if he were working in a zendo. By neatly, cleanly, silently and punctually preparing the food, he maintains a zazen atmosphere. Even more importantly, he wastes nothing. For instance, suppose he uses wood for cooking. If he saves a piece of wood each day, in one year he can save three hundred sixty-five pieces of wood. This "no waste" practice of the tenzo applies to everything, including electricity and water. Even an almost completely withered vegetable is revitalized and served.

During sesshin when the tenzo is good, the rest of the sesshin goes well. If he is sloppy we find it more difficult to go on. Working behind closed doors in the kitchen, although the tenzo himself remains inconspicuous, his work is most conspicuous, most influential. I am saying these things not to scare you, but rather to start you thinking about all that this practice entails.

"You young gaijin! You don't know what the practice is." And thus the elderly Chinese tenzo returned to his monastery.

What then is "the practice"? In the zendo you don't have to do anything except sit down on a cushion and erect your spine. Everything else is done for you. Even if you are just sitting there, daydreaming, cooking up some fancy thoughts, when 12:30 comes you will be fed. If, however, instead of cooking the rice, the tenzo starts cooking up wild fancies of his own, everybody would start to complain: "What is the matter with that tenzo?" But the tenzo never complains: "What is the matter with you there in the zendo?" Zazen is just one part of the practice, not all of it.

At this point, let me tell you another story. My teacher's teacher, Gempo Yamamoto Roshi, often told us that in whichever monastery he lived, he willingly volunteered to be tenzo. When he was the abbot of Ryutaku Monastery, a lay-student, Mr. Tanaka, came to stay for a while, wishing to participate in monastery life. This took place during an interim period, so most of the monks were away. Mr. Tanaka was asked to be tenzo. He was delighted to do so. Once Gempo Roshi came to the kitchen and said, "Hello, Mr. Tanaka. How are you?"

"Fine, thank you."

"Do you enjoy being tenzo?"

"Yes, I do."

"Why are you doing this?"

"I am doing this for all the monks and for all sentient beings."

Then Gempo Roshi left the kitchen.

A few days later Gempo Roshi came again. "Hello, Mr. Tanaka. How are you?"

"I am fine, thank you, Roshi!"

"Do you enjoy being tenzo?"

"Yes, I do."

"Why are you doing this?"

"I cook for all the monks and for all sentient beings."

And again, Gempo Roshi silently left.

A few days later: "Hello, Mr. Tanaka. How are you? How is your tenzo getting along?"

"Getting better and better."

"Why are you doing this?"

"For all the monks . . . ."

Gempo Roshi interrupted, "SHUT UP! Do not deceive yourself. You are doing this for *you*, for your practice and for your virtue!"

Again this story has many things to tell us, but it is up to each one of us how much we can get from it. Each person has different karma. Speaking about karma, particularly during sesshin, our true karma reveals itself. Let me tell you that it is crystal clear when you come to dokusan. We know that all people are basically alike: one face, two eyes, one nose, two nostrils, one mouth, one tongue, two ears, two hands, two legs. Yet each person is amazingly different. So different. Someone told me last night that upon hearing the verse of the *Diamond Sutra*:

> *I ssai u i ho*
> *Nyo mu gen ho yo*
> *Nyo ro yaku nyo den*
> *O sa nyo ze kan*

> *(All composite things are like a dream,*
> *A phantasm, a bubble and a shadow;*
> *Like a dewdrop and a flash of lightning—*
> *They are thus to be regarded.*)*

he truly understood THIS matter. And someone else, with the sound of yesterday's evening rain, truly understood. But just to say "understand" is not enough. It is far more than that. However, there is no equivalent word for such an experience, so we have to use the word "understand."

"They are thus to be regarded." Throughout sesshin there are the same people, eating the same food, sitting in the same zendo. But some are still thinking about the past. Some are still looking for outside help. Everyone is so very different.

Lately, I am thinking more and more that this practice which we are doing now is certainly not only for this one lifetime. We may spend twenty, thirty, forty, fifty or even sixty years of practice. But the karma of practice cannot be accumulated in such a short time. This is particularly true when we are attempting to accumulate karma in the practice of spiritual matters. Right now, some of you may have relatively weak karmic relations. But if we make the cause now as best we can, we can afford to let the Dharma worry about the effect.

* Translated by Dr. D. T. Suzuki

What is important to understand is that this practice is not only for this lifetime. It is a long-term project, but during this life, we are given the opportunity either to do our best, our medium or our rare. If that is understood, maybe that elderly Chinese monk would say, "Oh, you young gaijin! You now know what practice is." On the other hand, if we still think that sitting on a cushion in half-lotus or full-lotus position *is* our practice and only this sitting *is* important, our understanding of the direction is not clear.

Because of the transparent, extremely lucid atmosphere in the zendo, many mysterious things have been happening. They are "mysterious" only from the ordinary point of view. But from the point of view of deep samadhi, they are not at all mysterious. I will give you one example. One person in this zendo lost his voice about a month ago. Yesterday, while we were chanting the *Diamond Sutra*, his voice suddenly came back. We call this a miracle from the ordinary point of view, but we call it natural from the mysterious point of view. In any case, whatever it's called, I am very happy to be able to talk to him. So this afternoon, when you chant the *Diamond Sutra*, chant with all your might. When the mind is occupied with chanting or with Mu, there will be no pain. When the mind is occupied with pain, there will be no chanting and no Mu.

One of the reasons we chant the *Diamond Sutra* is because when Dai Bosatsu Zendo was still under construction, some financial problems arose. So we decided to chant the *Diamond Sutra* in order to appeal to the One Mind of the Universe. First we read it in English and then we just chanted. And later, because of this *sutra*, we named this temple Kongo-ji, Temple of Diamond. And now we still continue to chant it because of the karmic relation between the *Diamond Sutra* and Kongo-ji. Besides, the importance of chanting the *Diamond Sutra* has been emphasized by the various patriarchs, particularly Hui Neng (Eno Daikon Zenji), the Sixth Patriarch.

Always introductions are very long. The introduction is my teisho.

Some people consider themselves confused. If you think in this manner, let me ask you (from the *Diamond Sutra*):

Past mind cannot be grasped.

Present mind cannot be grasped.
Future mind cannot be grasped.

So, with which mind are you confused? Think about this matter.

All right, "Gutei's Finger" . . . this story contains three important points: Gutei always raised his finger; the boy was enlightened; the Master passed away saying, "I attained this finger Zen from my teacher, Tenryu, and although I have used it throughout my life, I could never use it up." I will begin my comments from this last part, namely, how did Gutei attain this finger Zen?

Gutei is not this master's real name. He was nicknamed Gutei because he was always chanting the *Gutei Dharani*. Gutei, who lived two generations after Baso Goitsu Zenji (709–88), dwelled in a small hut on a mountain, doing zazen and chanting by himself. One day a nun dressed for travel, wearing a bamboo hat and carrying a staff, entered Gutei's cottage. She walked around this room three times, stopped in front of Gutei and demanded, "Speak! (Say something to adequately express this so-called Ultimate Reality.) Speak! (Say something to express your Zen.)"

The nun's whole manner seemed rude and contemptuous. She did not even remove her hat, as common etiquette prescribed.

Gutei, intimidated, could not answer and he felt very ashamed of himself. Finally he said to her, "It's getting late. Please stay overnight."

"If you can speak, I will stay. If not, I will leave."

And again Gutei could not adequately express his empirical comprehension in his own way. The nun left.

Gutei felt so ashamed of himself that he decided to leave his hut in order to join a monastery and practice zazen until he could expand his consciousness, as it were. But that evening a protecting deity appeared to Gutei in a dream and said, "Wait, wait, don't leave. In a few days a living *bodhisattva* will come here."

So Gutei, although he had prepared his hat, his straw sandals and his bag, decided to wait. A few days later, a Zen master called Tenryu visited him. Receiving Tenryu in his hut, Gutei told the story about the nun who had visited him without even removing her hat.

"She walked around my room three times and then commanded me to speak. But I could not. As a student of Zen I feel so ashamed of myself." With all his might he begged Master Tenryu, "Please teach me."

Master Tenryu remained silent for a while. Gutei gazed at him singlemindedly. Then Tenryu raised his finger. Time was ripe—readiness of time—for Gutei. So with this raised finger as a strong stimulation, he was able to understand this condensed, indescribable, inexpressible THIS matter. Thus, throughout Gutei's life, whenever someone asked him about Zen, he would raise his finger.

Gutei's finger-teaching resembles the teaching of the Earth-Striking Master who responded to questions by striking the ground with his stick. Once someone took the Earth-Striking Master's stick and then asked him a question. Without hesitation he was able to respond. He shouted, "Ka-a-a! Ka-a-a!" Once someone opens his Mind's Eye, he knows how to express THIS under any circumstance. Aids like fingers and sticks are unnecessary. No hesitation! No imitation! No plastic Zen!

So Gutei attained finger Zen. And when he became old, evidently there was a young attendant monk who began to imitate him. When anyone asked the boy about his master's teachings, he would raise his finger. Gutei heard about the boy's mischief, seized him and cut off his finger. The boy cried and started to run away, but Gutei called after him.

"Stop! Turn around!"

When the young monk turned his head, Gutei raised his own finger. In that instant the monk was enlightened. In short, realized THIS matter.

Cutting off a finger, violence and blood are not at all the point of this story. Do not misunderstand! What appears here is the combination of "the readiness of time" and strong stimulation.

When Gutei was about to die, he gathered everybody together and said, "I have learned this finger Zen from Tenryu and I have used it throughout this lifetime. But I could not exhaust it."

When you do zazen you should do it with intense *nen*, "thought" or "mindfulness." But with this *nen* you should have one Great Vow. We are not only searching for our own contentment. The contentment which we seek is on a universal, international scale:

May we extend this mind over the whole universe,
So that we and all beings together
May attain maturiry in Buddha's wisdom.

With this vow, little by little, our dualistic, discriminating consciousness disappears and no longer do we think in terms of "koan and
me" or "I am doing this work" or "my practice is Mu" or "my koan
is this and that." Unless subject and object begin to approach each
other, become nearer to each other, there is no point in doing zazen.
Zazen is not a matter of entering into some kind of ecstasy or high.
Master Hakuin tells us:

Even those who have practiced it for just one sitting
Will see all their evil karma erased.

This statement is normally misunderstood. Most people think that
one sitting refers to one period of zazen, lasting some forty or forty-five
minutes. "So I did a few sittings today and some of my evil karma has
been erased." This is not that "one." Even those who have practiced
it for *Just One* sitting, one sitting of total *Oneness*—non-dualistic sitting—
will see all their evil karma erased.

There is One stone under the ocean. Pick it up without getting your
robe wet. One stone!

What is the sound of One hand? The sound of One hand!

One hand!

One stone!

ONE!

This is the Universal Samadhi, the Diamond Samadhi. If we are able
to do one melting zazen, One Melting Zazen, if we are able to do one
integrating sitting, One Integrating Sitting, all our evil karma cannot
but be erased.

That calligraphy of the Chinese character "Mu," which is hanging
on the wall, was written by a Dr. Hisamatsu who is now over eighty
years old. He is a Zen scholar and Zen man living in Kyoto, and he is
actually one of the original organizers of the Cambridge Buddhist
Society. That Mu is quite something. It could not have been written

without One Sitting. Mu wrote Mu. Mu painted Mu on Mu. Painted by Mu, for Mu, in Mu, on Mu—all kinds of prepositions. That Mu speaks as loud as thunder. It is Dr. Hisamatsu's One finger. A flower arrangement, the gong, the mokugyo, the clappers, the taste of the food, cleaning—each is a different "finger"—each has depth according to our practice. The sound of the kansho bell, which you strike before coming to dokusan, speaks most honestly of the depth of your practice. It is your finger Zen in sound.

The enlightenment which Gutei and the young monk attained has nothing to do with a finger. If you cling to the idea of a finger, Tenryu and Bodhidharma will be so disappointed. The finger is just a symbol as was Hyakujo's Fox and Joshu's Dog—just symbols.

Has a dog Buddha nature or not?

Has a fox Buddha nature or not?

Has a finger Buddha nature or not?

And we are expressing our own Buddha nature in everything that we do, everything that we think, everything that we speak, everything that we act. Especially in aesthetics, your choice of color, size, proportion and sound—these all express your Zen, originating from One Sitting, THIS Sitting.

It is not a matter of searching for tranquility or of attaining ecstasy or of becoming high. To learn to express your Zen, in your own way, is what zazen practice is all about. This is what we are doing here. We are not doing some other kind of meditation.

Dai Bosatsu Zendo Kongo-ji
September 9, 1976

Fuketsu's Speech and Silence

The Gateless Gate: Case 24

The Koan:

    A monk asked Fuketsu, "Both speech and silence are concerned with ri *and* bi. *How can you express the Truth without speaking, without silence?"*

    Fuketsu answered, "I always remember the South in March. While the partridge sings, hundreds of flowers exude their fragrance."

The Teisho:

It is a good karmic coincidence that today's teisho has something to do with spring. Officially it is not yet spring, but today is more than spring. Now we are feeling a certain sameness of mind. That is, there is a sameness: one life. One Mind. And yet, in appearance, we are all different.

As a preface to the teisho I will read my translation of a poem dedicated to Master Bassui. It was composed in Japanese by an anonymous poet. For various reasons I assume that the poet is Soen Roshi, but I do not know for sure.

In the translation the word "Salutations!" appears several times. The original expression is more than a greeting. It goes more or less like this:

> *With a reverential heart,*
> *My head at your feet,*
> *Devoting my life to you,*
> *Master Bassui Tokusho Zenji Dai Osho.*

The final dialogue, when Bassui says, "Wait, I will tell you when Dai Bosatsu Mountain makes great laughter," read "Mt. Fuji" rather than

"Dai Bosatsu Mountain" in the original text.

Master Bassui Tokusho Zenji (1327–87) was a Japanese Zen master. Not depending on the so-called old-fashioned, square Zen, he created his own way of teaching Zen practice. His "What is THIS?" and "Who is THIS?" are stimulating questions for us all.

Offering Poem:

> *Salutations to Master Bassui!*
> *Yellow skin and white skin,*
> *Red skin and black skin,*
> *Four billion people on this earth,*
> *Separate from one another.*
> *Sometimes with joy,*
> *At other times with sorrow;*
> *Sometimes with smiles,*
> *And other times in anger,*
> *Thus they spend their lives,*
> *Transmigration*
> > *after*
> > > *transmigration.*

> *Nevertheless, people believe*
> *There is nothing that cannot*
> > *be studied.*
> *From minutely small particles*
> *To the distant sun and stars,*
> *Philosophy and psychology,*
> *Medicine and physics,*
> *They study everything,*
> *And are proud of themselves.*

> *However, when the questions come,*
> *Who is actually studying?*
> *Who is the one who wants to study?*
> *How many people on this earth*
> *Can answer such questions, I wonder?*

As the blind baby does not know
The color of the milk,
Most people on this earth
Are blind in the Dharma,
Blind to the Dharma.
What a pity! What a danger!

Salutations to Master Bassui!
When True Dharma is almost disappearing,
You show us the great way to emancipation.
It is so clear.
I did my best
By chanting sutras, praying,
Pilgrimages and
Invoking the Buddha's name.
Sometimes only eating roots
And wild herbs,
Other times sitting long hours
Without rest, searching
For the true pacified Mind,
But never realizing
The one who is searching.
It is like steaming the sand
And waiting for the rice
To be cooked.

Salutations to Master Bassui!
"If you want to free yourself
From the suffering of birth and death,
You must learn the way
To become a Buddha.
The way to become a Buddha
Is no other than
Realizing your own Mind.
If you want to realize your own Mind,
You must first of all
Find the root

From which thoughts grow.
Whether sleeping or working,
Standing or sitting,
Continually ask yourself,
'What is my own Mind?'
With great yearning
Solve this question.
This is training.
This is practice.
This is determination.
Or it may be called
Thirst for enlightenment.
What is called zazen
Is no other than this
Seeing into your own Mind."

Following your instructions,
I practiced. "What is this Mind?"
"What is this Mind?"
Time and again,
Day and night.

To my amazement,
I saw the glittering light
In all existences
Revealing as my Mind.

"Whether you are monk or lay person,
So long as you continue to ask yourself,
'What is this Mind?'
Without fail,
You will attain something.
But if you do not practice in this way,
That something will never be appreciated."

Yes!
True indeed,

With great joy
I left the mountain.
In a few days, however,
My treasured Mind mirror
Again collected dust.
"Smash the mirror!"
Throwing enlightenment away
To return to the source,
I worked diligently,
Remembering your sayings:
"When thoughts vanish,
Self nature illumines
In the ten directions
Of the world,
And the joy
Of this condition
Cannot be described!"

You are quite right!

Salutations to Master Bassui!
Now, let me ask you,
"Has a dog Buddha nature
Or not?"
Joshu said, "Mu!"
What is this Mu?
You may answer,
"Wait, I will tell you
When Dai Bosatsu Mountain
Makes great laughter!"

By now, the destination of our practice is clear to everybody. All we are interested in is Mind. Mind! Nothing else!

According to Oriental thought, the mind has at least three elements or functions: *chi, jo,* and *i. Chi* means "wisdom," *jo* means "emotions," that is, the ability to feel emotions, and *i* may be translated as "consciousness," the ability to judge right and wrong, or "will power."

The purpose of our zazen is, first of all, to make sure that our wisdom works properly, that is, to make sure that our *jo* is sensitive enough to react, and to make sure that our *i* is always accurate and strong. Let us cultivate our minds and make use of our minds, instead of being used by our minds.

The best part of Mu practice is that it is so direct, so powerful. But there is the danger of its becoming mechanical repetition, repeating Mu after Mu without thinking why or what . . . . Now, thinking and thoughts are two different matters as far as zazen practice is concerned. What is not good is to have miscellaneous thoughts during zazen. But pure thinking for koan study is equivalent to intensive concentration on Mu. We must think deeply.

Now today's koan: A monk asked Fuketsu Ensho Zenji (896–975), the fourth generation Dharma successor of Rinzai Gigen Zenji, "Since both speech and silence are concerned with *ri* and *bi*, how can you express the Truth (or how can you express Mu) without speaking and without silence?"

Ri actually means "equality" and *bi* means "differentiation." For example, when we are silent, we have equality in silence. This is ri. The plain fact is: equality is Mind, the One Mind, and this Mind is no other than ri. But when we are allowed to speak, we differentiate ourselves with our talk. This is bi. Appearance and personality are different for each person. This is bi. Therefore, neither silence nor words can express the Truth. Silence is limited to ri and language is limited to bi. Thus the monk was asking a rather difficult question: "Without speaking, without silence, how do you express the Truth?"

Master Fuketsu, without hesitation, said, "I always remember the South in March. The partridges sing, hundreds of flowers exude their fragrance."

Some of you may think, "Oh, that is speaking." You may remember this very well-known koan: "Pick up the hoe and cultivate the ground without using your hands." This is the same as saying: "Pick up your chopsticks and eat lunch without using your hands." Try it today. Actually, every day you are doing this very beautifully. Maybe some of you think that your chopstick-holding condition is not as good as the person's sitting next to you. But most of us are not aware that we are using our hands. We are not aware that we are using chopsticks. And yet, the plain fact is: we are using them and, at the same time, we are not aware of it.

Last spring I went to Washington, D. C., to see the cherry blossoms. As they were so breathtaking, I had to say, "Wow! Beautiful!"

Now, is this silence or speech?

Here is another example. Until we have stomach problems most of us are not aware that our stomach works very hard every day. "Ah, I should have taken care of it more carefully. I smoked too much and drank too much." Too late now for such regrets! When even one finger is hurt and we are inconvenienced, then all of a sudden we realize the existence of that finger. But until that time, we were not aware of it. It was as if we had never used it. So, in the same way, during zazen whether we are counting our breath, working on Mu or shikantaza, or whatever, when we are with it, "without words, without silence," this itself is a beautiful manifestation of Mu. This is true, but still some of you may think that Mu must be somewhere else. You may think that to realize Mu must be something very dramatic. Heaven and earth must turn upside down. These are all superfluous thoughts.

So, what we have to do is to continue to dig. Dig with Mu! Dig with breath counting! Dig! Dig your mind! Dig and think! (Pure thinking —not pursuing miscellaneous thoughts.) Dig it?

Do your zazen dynamically! Become your zazen! Become your life!

There are two elements which we need to cultivate: dynamism and elegance. By cultivating elegance I mean simplifying and refining the quality of our lives. But we cannot have dynamic and elegant lives without discovering the refined quality of Mind. Appreciate Master Fuketsu's wonderful response to the monk's rather perverse question. "I always remember the South in March while the partridge sings, hundreds of flowers exude their fragrance!"

Dai Bosatsu Zendo Kongo-ji
March 6, 1977

Baso, Chizo, Ekai

The Blue Rock Collection: Case 73

The Koan:

A monk asked the great Master Baso, "Separating ourselves from the four affirmations and cutting ourselves off from the hundred negations, please tell me clearly, what was the reason for Bodhidharma coming to China?"

Baso said, "Today I am very tired and I cannot explain this to you. Go and get an answer from Chizo!"

So the monk went to Chizo and asked him the same question.

Chizo said, "Why did you not ask Master Baso?"

"I did, and he told me to come to you."

Chizo said, "Today I have a headache and cannot explain the matter to you . Go and ask Ekai!"

So the monk went to Ekai who said, "I do not understand that sort of question."

When the monk went back to Baso and told him the whole story, Baso said, "Isn't Chizo's head white? Isn't Ekai's head black?"

The Teisho:

Only one day's zazen has already changed the atmosphere of the zendo. The atmosphere of the zendo is being created by all the participants in this sesshin. Just one day of zazen has changed our Mind. Master Hakuin said,

> *As for zazen practice in the Mahayana,*
> *We have no words to praise it fully.*

In the past I have spoken to you about the difference between teisho and lecture, but today I will try to do it again. So, before we go into the koan, let me give you some kind of introductory remarks. Naturally these remarks will become a lecture, not a teisho.

The transmission of the Dharma does not require any written document. The only important matter is to understand the real nature of the universe. In order to do this, it will be helpful to understand the distinction between *honbun* and *shusho*. Unless these are clearly distinguished, only confusion arises. We have no perfect English equivalent for these words, but perhaps "fundamental" or "essential" will do for honbun. For shusho, perhaps we can translate it as "existential" or "ever-changing."

I will use the wind to illustrate the difference between honbun and shusho. Whether the wind is a fragrant spring wind, or a cold winter wind, or just a gentle wind, after all, the wind is merely a movement of air. Metaphorically speaking, honbun (fundamental) refers to this air and shusho (existential) is the changing condition of the wind.

Our True Nature, our Endless Dimension Universal Nature, was never created and can never be destroyed, as far as honbun goes.

In the realm of honbun, there is no loss, no gain, no birth, no death, no good, no evil, no small, no large. But as far as shusho is concerned, as you can see, there is strong and weak, coming and going, deep and shallow. Thus in our zazen we often feel different conditions.

Sometimes we think, "Today's zazen is not as good as yesterday's." Or, "I feel guilty because my zazen is not as good as it should be." Or, "I am very pleased that I have entered some sound samadhi." Most of us are fooled by these thoughts. We are controlled by ever-changing conditions. We become slaves of conditions. Realization of Mu (True Nature) means to realize the fact that the fundamental Mu nature is far beyond good or bad, deep or shallow. This is honbun.

The chanting of *Namu Dai Bosa* is another example of the fact that, fundamentally speaking, we are all Dai Bosa, enlightened beings. Not only we human beings, but also all sentient beings are primarily, fundamentally enlightened. This not only applies to all beings, but also the bowing mat, the broken chopstick, the sick cat—all are enlightened beings. To put it in a more comprehensible way, they are absolutely all right as they are. In fact, everything is all right as it is. At this moment, a fine bowl is all right as a fine bowl. If it is broken, it is all right as a broken bowl, and if it is fixed, it is all right as a repaired bowl. The fact is that everything is all right as it is, and, in fact, cannot be otherwise—this is *Namu Dai Bosa*. Some of us have already testified to this, but if you have not yet done so, at least believe it. You must believe it!

As for the chanting of *Namu Dai Bosa*, sometimes we can chant it very smoothly. We can go with it. Other times, to chant even one *Namu Dai Bosa* is too difficult to finish without interrupting thoughts. Still other times, we may find ourselves in *Namu Dai Bosa* chanting samadhi for half a day. But these are just conditions.

Remember that the conditions are constantly changing, depending on your physical, mental, and emotional states. Don't be deluded by conditions. "Today my *Namu Dai Bosa* is bad." "Today my *Namu Dai Bosa* is good." This is fine as a report of condition, but don't forget that *Namu Dai Bosa* is always all right, regardless of the condition. It is always as it is!

The inseparability and, at the same time, the clear distinctiveness of honbun and shusho is the factuality of the universe, existing even before the creation of heaven and earth. This is not particularly a religious concept, nor is it a specialty of Zen Buddhism—it is a plain fact. But in the tradition of Mahayana Buddhism, it is emphasized time and again to realize Fundamental Reality, as we human beings have a tendency to look at only one aspect—that is, the existential, ever-changing condition of phenomena. We have a tendency to miss seeing the other fundamental aspect.

The two appear simultaneously, not like the famous saying, "two sides of a coin." This is a wonderful expression, but when we see one side of the coin, we cannot see the other side. The fundamental and existential aspects of phenomena are appearing right now, simultaneously, like water (honbun) and wave (shusho). Nothing is hidden! And consequently, nothing need be uncovered! So from the honbun point of view, birds sing—that is the birds' teisho; chrysanthemums bloom silently—that is the chrysanthemums' teisho; a candle burns, dust moves, gongs gong! From day to night there are millions of instruments playing in the Dharma orchestra. Once we are able to realize this fact, we know that whether we are going or returning, sitting or not sitting, we are the Dharma itself. So, let us make very clear that we are not searching for something outside, and we are not trying to uncover something concealed. Rather, we are working for the realization of that which is already revealed. But it is so close and so familiar to us, our habit of emphasizing existential phenomena is so strong, and our judgment of good and bad is so deeply rooted that it is difficult for us to appreciate this wonderful Dharma teaching.

Now back to today's koan. I remember that Hakuun Yasutani Roshi once said, just before giving a teisho on this koan, "If all of you make your minds, right now, like a sheet of white paper and listen very carefully, then by the end of the teisho, everybody will be enlightened."

The story goes like this, "A monk went to Master Baso." It is said that Baso Doitsu Zenji (709–88) had over three hundred Dharma successors. That's quite a few! Baso must have been more than just a skillful teacher. He must have had great virtue and many good students, otherwise he couldn't have had so many successors.

One day a traveling monk, whose name remains unknown, went to Master Baso and spoke to him using some complicated expressions. Actually, what he was saying was, "Please do not use any kind of philosophical explanations, but tell me, why did Bodhidharma come from India to China?" Or, "Without using any philosophical terms, please tell me what is the essence of Zen Buddhism—Truth itself?"

Baso said, "Today I am tired. Why don't you go to my student, Chizo, and ask him about it?"

Maybe Baso was really exhausted. But here is illustrated what I meant when I said that the two aspects are two and yet are one, simultaneously. Exhaustion is the existential condition of the body. "Today I am tired." "Today I am fine." "Today . . . whatever." "Today I *am*" is the essential condition and that is no other than the essence of Zen Buddhism. So this is what Baso is really saying. He just used normal conversation. "I am tired. Go and ask my student, Chizo."

Now look, some of you are tired right now; some of you look sleepy; some of you look very serious; some of you seem very confused; some of you are very excited. But just by being as you are, all of you are giving the answer to this traveling monk.

However, this traveling monk obviously interpreted Baso's answer existentially. He may have thought to himself, "This teacher must be getting old. He cannot even answer my question. Maybe he's too busy and cannot spare any time for me." So the monk went to Master Chizo and asked the same question. Chizo said, "Why didn't you go to my master?"

By this time you know the existential interpretation of this answer very well. "Why didn't you go to my master?"—this is the perfect answer as it is. There is no such thing as the essence of Dharma or the essence of Ultimate Reality apart from here and now. Somehow we think that there is something hidden, as the monk was thinking when he said, "Well, I did, I went." By saying so he is answering his own question. "I did." But still he did not understand, so Chizo kindly said, "I have a headache today. Go to Ekai."

The traveling monk by now must have been very confused. "The master is exhausted, the second one has a headache; what will be with the third one?" He went to Ekai and asked the same question. Ekai said, "I don't understand this sort of question."

The traveling monk must have thought, "What's going on here? An exhausted master, a headachy teacher, an ignorant brother monk!" So, finally he went back to Baso again to report. Then the master very kindly said, "Wasn't Chizo's head white? Wasn't Ekai's head black?" Baso could have also said, "Wasn't Chizo tall? Wasn't Ekai fat?" But time was not yet ready for the monk, so he was unable to realize the reality.

Normally, most koans end with the monks becoming enlightened. This monk was not enlightened, but it's nice to have it this way once in a while.

We always tend to shift the emphasis from one extreme to the other. We are one-sided—either we look at phenomena fundamentally, or we look at them existentially. But fundamental is existential and vice versa. Like yin and yang, they cannot be separated.

We are already enlightened. We cannot be enlightened any more. But, we can sit more mindfully. We can realize this *fact* more clearly. Let's do our best.

Dai Bosatsu Zendo Kongo-ji
May 10, 1975

Beardless Bodhidharma

The Gateless Gate: Case 4

The Koan:

Wakuan said, "Why has Bodhidharma no beard?"

Mumon's Comment:

If you want to practice Zen, you must practice it with your whole heart. When you attain realization, it must be True Realization. The great Bodhidharma can be seen only when you become him. Just one glimpse will be enough. But if you say that you have seen him, you have never seen him at all.

The Teisho:

Wakuan said, "Why has Bodhidharma no beard?" At this point I don't think that it is so essential for us to spend time introducing Wakuan. Just remember that he was a Zen master of the Sung Dynasty. His full name was Wakuan Shitai Zenji and he lived from 1108 until 1179.

But Bodhidharma must be introduced.

Buddhism was born in India some twenty-five hundred years ago. The Zen Buddhist tradition has been continually transmitted from teacher to Dharma heir since the time of the Buddha himself. Bodhidharma was the twenty-eighth patriarch (Dharma heir) in India and the first patriarch in China. He traveled all the way from India to China to introduce Buddha-Dharma to the Chinese people. As far as readiness of time is concerned, India was ready to transmit the Buddha-Dharma, but China was not yet ready to receive it. It was the middle of the sixth century. Nowadays, North America is ready to receive it and Japan, Tibet and some countries of Southeast Asia are ready to send it.

During Bodhidharma's time evidently China was not ready for Zen Buddhism. Various schools of intellectual Buddhism were predominant. Realizing the unreadiness of time, Bodhidharma went to the northern part of China and stayed in a monastery called Shorin-ji for nine years—just sitting, waiting for the readiness of time, radiating his samadhi vibration throughout the land. And while he was sitting, naturally his beard grew and therefore all the paintings of Bodhidharma depict him with a beard and great, wide-open eyes. Nonetheless, Wakuan is asking us, "Why has Bodhidharma no beard?"

This is the unique part of Zen Buddhism. Wakuan's question stresses the importance of intuitive understanding rather than analytical comprehension. But sometimes analysis is interesting, so let me try. The name Bodhidharma is first of all interesting. *Bodhi* means "enlightened" and *dharma* means "Ultimate Reality." I will come back to this point later, but first let me say something about zazen.

Now when we do deep zazen, we forget about time. On the other hand, when the condition is not good, ten minutes may seem like one hour. So when we are in this deep condition, melting into the cushion . . . into the floor . . . into the earth . . . into the surrounding air . . . into ourselves—this condition of zazen can be called "unseparated feeling."

But most of the time, when one sitting is so wonderful the following sitting isn't as good. Attachment to samadhi is the impediment. Anticipation is the obstruction. Attachment, expectation—these are parts of human nature. It is pointless to say that you must not be attached, that you must not anticipate anything. But we should know that it is this condensed, intense mental energy, created by anticipation and attachment, that blocks the smooth flow of the breath. It takes time to be free. But one day we will reach a point when we can just say, "It doesn't matter." Good zazen or bad zazen, deep, continuous samadhi or shallow, inconsistent samadhi—"It doesn't matter." This is what I mean when I speak about transcending. And it is at this point that we can testify to the taste of Zen. This takes a long time.

Speaking about a long time, the Way to Dai Bosatsu, that is, the Way to Bodhisattvahood, is long, indeed long. But the fact is, we are already on that very Way! We have already started walking on it. In this sense it is not at all a long time.

It is very important for us to realize these two aspects of our zazen practice: the fact that the Way is endless and the fact that we are already on the Way. If we forget about the latter, we may be constantly looking for an endless end, not paying any attention to this present being.

Whether our zazen is so-called good, so-called bad, so-called deep or so-called shallow, we are still on the Way. Don't become too attached to the various conditions of your zazen. These conditions are simply manifestations of such things as your health, your temperament, the weather, and so on. As the *Diamond Sutra* tells us, "past mind is ungraspable." Past zazen is equally ungraspable. So forget everything and just do Mu!

Often people call Zen Buddhism a creative religion. Indeed it is creative. Each minute we create something new. And on each occasion we apply that new creativity.

Some people call Zen Buddhism a religion of universality. Yes, it is. It was practiced in India, China, Japan and now in America. It is and was practiced by people of various religions, cultural and racial backgrounds. In other words, no one is excluded from the practice of Zen, and no one need convert to the religion of Buddhism.

When we go into a deep condition of zazen, when we have kensho, this is a very important experience. In order to avoid conceptualizations and attachments, I deliberately do not stress the experience of kensho. So I often say, "Just do Mu, Mu, Mu . . . !" This is more important than kensho. Walk! Walk! Walk! Walk on the Way to Dai Bosatsu. Just go ahead! March on! March on! And you'll see what you'll see!

What is kensho? *Ken* means "to see" or "to realize." *Sho* means "nature." We see our own Nature. We see the Nature of the universe. This is kensho. So when we have kensho experience, indeed this world is Bodhi-Dharma, Enlightened Ultimate Reality. In this world there are no "beards," no right or wrong, no bad or good, no attainment or loss. Normally we have many kinds of "beards." Indeed Bodhi-Dharma is beardless! This is one very important point. But it seems that Wakuan is not pointing to this fundamental Bodhi-Dharma. Rather he is speaking about an historical figure: Bodhidharma Dai Shi Dai Osho, with his beard.

"Why has Bodhidharma no beard?" As long as this statement is used in the practice of zazen, as long as it is called a koan, we must forget about history and historical significance. During zazen we become Bodhidharma. Zazen practice is the practice of *becoming*.

To understand this koan, we must train ourselves to become Bodhidharma, just Bodhidharma and nothing else. During the sitting become Bodhidharma! Do not search for Bodhidharma somewhere else, but become, identify yourself with and melt into Bodhidharma. When we are speaking about mountains, become a mountain. When we are speaking about stones, become a stone. And if this training is done well, when we go back to society, we can face our various problems. A Zen master said:

> *Shiver when it's cold!*
> *Sweat when it's hot!*

However, instead of shivering, we turn on the heating system. Instead of sweating, we turn on the air conditioner. And when these devices are out of order, we complain, we become angry. And when oil is no longer available, we are in trouble. The practice of becoming when we are in trouble is to become the trouble itself. When you are in Rome, as the saying goes, do as the Romans. This is easy to say, but . . . . We are always thinking about ways to avoid problems or about how to solve problems by taking some action, instead of by becoming. What we can learn through zazen is the practice of becoming, becoming, becoming, more and more become, become! When you become a teacher, do what teachers do! When you become a student, do what students do! When you do zazen, do zazen and nothing else!

In the ordinary sense of becoming, we think in terms of becoming the President of the United States. In this case, in order to become, the President has to be nominated and elected. Only by relying on many other people's efforts can he become President.

This is not what I am talking about. Become—by your own nomination, by your own commitment. And that practice will become like our own flesh and blood and will be with us for the rest of our lives, wherever we go, whatever we do. And this is the benefit of direct experience. So zazen teaches us to become Mu, become the koan, become become, become . . .! No transformations! Just become!

Try to become Bodhidharma and ask yourself the question: "Why has Bodhidharma no beard?" Become Bodhidharma's mind. And once you have become Bodhidharma's mind you may become a stone's mind, a tree's mind, a finger's mind, a dog's mind, a cat's mind and, most importantly, become your Mind! Then you will understand Wakuan's question.

We are very skillful at diversifying things, but we are not so skillful at unifying things. Zazen is not a practice of diversity. It is a practice of feeling and realizing unity.

And Mumon's comment: "If you want to practice Zen, you must practice it with your whole heart." You must practice it not only with your whole heart, but also with your soul, with your body, with your mind—totally!

"When you attain realization, it must be True Realization." Here I should like to tell you how Soen Roshi and Gempo Roshi met. By the way, Gempo Roshi was about forty years older than Soen Roshi, his successor. Gempo Roshi was an *unsui* (a monk in a monastery) until he was nearly fifty years old. He started very late. In any case, Gempo Roshi used to conduct zazen meetings in Tokyo. Soen Roshi's ordination teacher had another Zen group nearby. One day their *keisaku* broke and Soen Roshi was sent to borrow another one at Gempo Roshi's place. At Gempo Roshi's zazen meeting, he had enough time to stay and hear that teacher's teisho. He was very impressed. After that Soen Roshi went every day to listen to the teishos. He'd just sit some place, listening inconspicuously. One day, he sat right in front of Gempo Roshi and it was on that day that Gempo Roshi read, with great spirit, this part of Mumon's comment:

If you want to practice Zen, you must practice it with your whole heart.
When you attain realization, it must be True Realization.

With this, Soen Roshi decided to become Gempo Roshi's student.

We are unable to figure out these karmic relationships with our limited brain. Some mysterious karma is just moving. Dai Bosatsu

Zendo was dedicated on July 4th, America's Bicentennial Day, and indeed this was a landmark day for the transmission of Buddha-Dharma from East to West—a landmark day for this special practice called zazen. But so far our history in America is very short. We haven't as yet established a long tradition. To transmit the tradition takes a long time and needs many people's efforts. Thank you for your effort.

Dai Bosatsu Zendo Kongo-ji
September 10, 1976

Tozan's Flax

The Gateless Gate: Case 18

The Koan:
A monk asked Tozan, "What is Buddha?"
Tozan said, "Three pounds of flax!"

Mumon's Comment:
Master Tozan understood Zen. He opened himself like a clam to show his insides. Let me ask you this question: at what point do you see Tozan's Zen?

The Verse:
> *Complete revelation! Three pounds of flax!*
> *Wonderful expression, but the meaning is far*
>   *more wonderful.*
> *Whoever talks about right and wrong,*
> *Is the very one who is right and wrong.*

The Teisho:
We often say, "It was a good sesshin." Do you know why? It is because of our zazen. And why does our zazen make sesshin good? It is because of our Mind. Why does our Mind make good zazen and good sesshin? It is because by nature our True Mind is good. And because of this there is hope for humanity.

Already today is the fifth day of Rohatsu Sesshin. There are many different ways to participate in sesshin. One is to attend without any obligations or responsibilities. Another way is to act as one of the officers who run sesshin. This is a subtle operation. The officers are required to pay really careful attention and therefore we may think that to be an officer during sesshin must interfere with zazen. On the contrary, what actually happens is no interference. The more attentive we are to various things, the clearer the movement of the wheel of the Dharma becomes. "Let no thought be wasted over it." An attentive attitude reflects on our sitting.

One of the officers said to me in amazement, "How subtly my usual mind is changing. Yet on a superficial level, it is as if nothing has happened." So to attend sesshin as a host or hostess is more effective than attending as a guest. A new dimension is somehow opened. For instance, vegetables are cut every day. But during sesshin, the tenzo, thinking of the sangha, cuts them more mindfully. That is why, when we eat, the vegetables look more alive, more beautiful, more fresh and more ready to offer themselves. We are able to see the True nature of vegetables. Also, especially during sesshin, we can discover that even the gong has its own nature. It prefers to be struck in a certain way. When we pay attention to the nature of things, our total view of life becomes wider.

Now, those who are not acting as officers during sesshin should pay attention to turning inward. This is simply not a question of attentive concentration. Rather, when we do zazen inwardly, intensively, we come to know that we are on the right Path. Sit with unfixed, soft, dynamic, fresh motivation. Sit without expectation. And consequently, something may happen, someday. Actually, everything is happening every day. It is just that we are not aware of it.

So, just sit! But as soon as I say, "just sit," the expression becomes a wilted conceptualization. It hardens and becomes fixed within our minds. What we have to do is restore its vitality, bring it back to life. Prepare your zazen with deep breathing. Complete exhalation. Keep yourselves, your motivation, and your zazen soft! With this understanding JUST SIT! With this understanding, continue Mu practice.

In the beginning, all traditions and rituals arose spontaneously; that is, they were absolutely suitable under particular circumstances. They were created pragmatically. Such spontaneously created rituals were performed formally, but with spirit. However, soon the rituals and traditions became conceptualized, and the original spirit, derived from the place and the moment, was lost. Only the corpse of formality was carried on. If we are obliged to act according to traditions and rituals, how can we become productive, creative and spontaneous human beings? There is no other way but to sit zazen. Do not think that zazen is one of these empty corpses. When we sit, our intuition acts all by itself. Spontaneity comes all by itself. It cannot be forced. But ironically, spontaneity needs some kind of preparation. In our case, zazen gives us the necessary preparation.

Today's koan: A monk asked Tozan, "What is Buddha?"

"Three pounds of flax!"

What is Buddha? The term "buddha" represents various ideas depending on how it is used. Etymologically speaking, the Sanskrit word *buddha* is a common noun meaning "enlightened one." Religiously speaking, when a devotee of Buddhism makes an offering to a particular artistic representation of a buddha, *i.e.*, a statue, he is showing his respect either to the historic Buddha or to one of the buddhas who dwell in the various buddha realms. Theoretically speaking, according to the basic tenet of Mahayana Buddhism, "all beings are primarily Buddha," and this all-pervasive Buddha appears as a function of the Dharmakaya. In other words, this is the Endless Dimension Universal Life Buddha, another name for Mu, another name for Mind.

So, as I explain the various buddhas, the word "Buddha" becomes more familiar to us. At the same time, it grows more vague. Yet it is a most important term for us as long as we declare ourselves to be Zen Buddhists. We must know what Buddha is, and therefore we must ask, "What is Buddha?" In *The Gateless Gate*, this question appears at least four times. It also appears commonly in *The Blue Rock Collection* and in many other Zen texts. Here are some typical dialogues:

"What is Buddha?"
Tozan said, "Three pounds of flax!"

"What is Buddha?"
Ummon answered, "Toilet paper!"

"What is Buddha?
Baso answered, "This very mind is the Buddha!"

There are so many different answers to the same question. But today I should like to examine Tozan's three pounds of flax.

Lately I have been thinking that there are only two matters essential for us. The first is taking refuge in the Three Treasures: Buddha, Dharma and Sangha. The second is the Great Vows for All:

> However innumerable all beings are,
> I vow to enlighten them all;
> However inexhaustible my delusions are,
> I vow to extinguish them all;
> However immeasurable the Dharma Teachings are;
> I vow to master them all;
> However endless the Buddha's Way is,
> I vow to follow it.

The first of the Three Treasures, Buddha, may be interpreted according to history. In this case Buddha refers to Buddha Shakyamuni Dai Osho, the man who was named Siddhartha Gautama and who lived in India some twenty-five hundred years ago. The Dharma is the teachings of the Buddha which are recorded in the sutras and the shastras. The Sangha includes the direct students of the Buddha as well as all the great patriarchs and teachers of the lineage. The broadest interpretation includes even ourselves because we are also practicing the Buddha's teachings and so are part of the continuing transmission.

The second way of interpreting the meaning of the Three Treasures is broader. When we refer to the Buddha as the Enlightened One, we must also take into account that there have been quite a few enlightened beings who did not know of Buddha's teachings. Jesus Christ was one. Also there were Confucius, Lao Tzu, Ramakrishna, and in the West, Socrates, Emerson, Beethoven and Shakespeare, among others. When we consider these people as Buddhas, we must also say that the *Analects of Confucius*, the *Tao Te Ching*, the Bible, the symphonies of Beethoven, the sonnets of Shakespeare, etc., are all Dharma. The Sangha thus includes all believers of a particular teaching that originated with a living Buddha. So if we apply this interpretation to Christianity, we may say that Jesus is the Buddha, the Bible is the

Dharma and all Christians are the Sangha.

Finally, a third interpretation of the Three Treasures relates to today's koan. In the question "What is Buddha?" Buddha means the Endless Dimension Universal Life, or that which is unnameable. But even the unnameable is sometimes called Dharmakaya, Ultimate Reality and so forth. Even to call it "unnameable" is naming it. The Dharma of this Buddha is all phenomena: trees, oceans, rivers, people, buildings, birds, planes and all other things of this world. All phenomena were born due to a minutely subtle combination of various causes and effects. So this Dharma, having begun a long time ago, continues even now and will continue tomorrow and every tomorrow thereafter. We are in the midst of this Dharma even though we may not be aware of it. We are like fish that are not aware of the ocean which surrounds them.

The Sangha of this third category is best described by the expression: "I see you in me, me in you." This being the case, Sangha includes all things, be they sentient or otherwise. A piece of paper, a drop of water, a peanut butter sandwich—all are Sangha members. Excluding nothing, no thing, this Sangha continually radiates. Keeping this non-exclusive, radiating Sangha in mind, it is a mistake to think: "My zazen is good," "My samadhi is important," or "I should accumulate more samadhi power without giving it up." During zazen, the more you radiate out, the better you can sit. The more you empty yourself, the more space is made for Mu to enter.

Our minds behave so strangely. We usually think that we want to receive something. Such thoughts only serve to create an even thicker ego-wall. It is best to radiate in order to create high-quality zazen, high-quality Mu. If everyone in this zendo would radiate the highest-quality Mu—radiate in his or her own way and pervade equally—we would all be able to open the gate. But when someone continues to hold onto his personal, precious samadhi, as such, he will miss the Great Samadhi which is there in front of him, to the left and right of him and in back of him. If you love yourself, offer yourself. If you don't love yourself, all right, hold onto your own tiny samadhi.

"Three pounds of flax!.' Tozan's answer doesn't have to be three pounds of flax. Perhaps at that particular moment Tozan was weighing some flax, so "three pounds of flax" spontaneously became the expression of his experience. "Three pounds of flax" is a wonderful answer for those who understand. It is a strange answer for those who do not understand.

Let me read Mumon's comment, which is really self-explanatory.

Master Tozan understood Zen. He opened himself like a clam to show his insides.
Let me ask you this question: at what point do you see Tozan's Zen?

The Verse:
Complete revelation! Three pounds of flax!
Wonderful expression, but the meaning is far more wonderful.
Whoever talks about right and wrong,
Is the very one who is right and wrong.

"Complete revelation!" Mu is completely revealed above you, in front of you, in back of you, to the left and right of you, below you, and inside of you. Mu is not somewhere else. Mu is not concealed. Mu is close enough.

"Whoever talks about right and wrong is the very one who is right and wrong." Whoever attaches himself to the three pounds of flax (or rice or whatever) is, as the Beatles call him, the "real nowhere man."

Let me tell you a story. Yasutani Roshi was the principal of a primary school. Teachers in that school were always talking about each other. They would constantly complain and criticize each other. Finally Yasutani Roshi wrote, "Whoever talks about right and wrong is the very one who is right and wrong," and posted it in front of his office. After that, the teachers stopped coming to him to complain.

New York Zendo Shobo-ji
January 19, 1977

Ummon's Toilet Paper

The Gateless Gate: Case 30

The Koan:

> Ummon was asked, "What is Buddha?"
> Ummon said, "Toilet paper!"

The Teisho:

Today I will begin the teisho by telling you a story from Dostoevski's *The Record of the House of the Dead*. There were prisoners and they were asked to do a great task. This task was a very strange one: they had to destroy a mountain and carry the dirt from one place to another. When the mountain was completely leveled, the prisoners were then made to carry the dirt back again to the spot where the mountain had originally stood. After they were ordered to do this the prisoners started to commit suicide. They could not find any meaning in their labor. At first they had thought that they were doing something for the purpose of some kind of construction work. This idea made them feel more agreeable toward their chores. But just to carry the dirt back and forth. . . .

Let me tell you another story which happened recently in Japan. Because of the chemicals thrown into the ocean by many factories, the fish in a certain area were all poisoned and could not be eaten. But the fishermen around that area continued to fish. The chemical company sent their trucks to the fish market and bought all the fish, only to throw them away somewhere else—not in the ocean. At first this didn't bother the fishermen. They were still getting paid. But after a while the fishermen started to have doubts about what they were doing. They were fishing the poison, not the fish. One fisherman said, "We used to feel good about our job because the fish were consumed by the people." Finally they stopped fishing altogether. Both the prisoners in Dostoevski's story and the Japanese fishermen had lost the purpose of their labor.

Now these two stories should make us think about what we are doing here. Zazen practice requires great labor—getting up early in the morning, sitting all day, fighting against drowsiness, enduring leg pain. In order to sit, in order to continue the practice, we need great faith. But if that were all we needed, sooner or later we would end up like the fishermen and the prisoners. Most importantly, we need to sit with Bodhisattva spirit; that is, sitting with the vow to serve and to save all beings. Most of you understand this Bodhisattva sitting theoretically. But if our batteries are charged only with theory, they will soon run dry. On the other hand, the battery of experience lasts a long, long time.

The other day, quite spontaneously during zazen practice, we all bowed nine times. With each bow we chanted:

> *All the evil karma ever committed by me since of old,*
> *On account of my beginningless greed, anger and folly,*
> *Born of my body, mouth and thought—*
> *I now confess and purify them all.*

The second bow was stronger than the first; the third was more power-ful; the fourth was more with it; the fifth was more concentrated. There is no theoretical reason for bowing nine times. With each bow, with our own effort, we created our own reason. One of the partici-pants later told me, "Now I know that to purify myself is no other than to purify all other beings." This is what I call charging our batteries with experience.

There is an expression which goes: "When one is enlightened, all others are enlightened." We have a hard time believing this because we know that even when someone has a kensho experience, all other beings are not enlightened. We think, "I am not enlightened, but he is." This kind of rationalizing is all right, but I have to call it the bumpkin's viewpoint. The bumpkin's viewpoint comes about when we deal with theories. Only when one has had the experience of en-lightenment is he able to truly say, "All others are also enlightened."

This is the most unique part of our practice. We do not study dogma. There is no such thing as dogmatic Zen, dogmatic kensho. We speak so often about this experience or that experience that this wonderful word "experience" has lost its impact. Any experience, worthy of being called experience, should be vital and dynamic. When it happens for the first time, you may be extremely impressed.

Most of us are familiar with the many talents of Master Hakuin. He was a great calligrapher and painter; he was an able organizer and made a new path to Rinzai Zen Buddhism; he was the author of *The Iron Kettle* and many other books, essays and poems, including *The Song of Zazen*. But, in fact, his greatest talent was that he was able to express, both comprehensibly and poetically, this experience. In *The Song of Zazen* Hakuin praises zazen and insists on the importance of its practice. Describing the content of zazen, he concludes this great work by saying:

> *How boundless the cleared sky of samadhi!*
> *How transparent the perfect moonlight of the Fourfold Wisdom!*
> *At this moment what more need we seek?*
> *As the Truth eternally reveals itself,*
> *This very place is the Lotus Land of Purity,*
> *This very body is the Body of the Buddha.*

What more can we say? But because we read this so often, we recite it like puppets and lose our appreciation for it. With the body-breath, with each inhalation and exhalation, we can thoroughly appreciate the real joy of being human. Indeed, "what more need we seek?" What more need we want?

Most of us have some preconceived notions about zazen practice. "I am seeking true freedom," "I am eager to become enlightened," "I would like to enter samadhi" . . . . Nothing is wrong with this kind of thinking. Just be sure that each time you start to do zazen, you remember that every day is different—every day is a new day! Samadhi is wonderful, if it comes. Kensho is fine, if it comes. The Way is always dynamic and vital, ready to be realized. Therefore all we need do is sit without ceasing.

Normally we speak only about this, our present life. Certainly some of our friends impress us as if they were born as human beings for the first time. Sometimes you may meet someone who acts as if he were a reincarnation of an animal, even though he speaks human language, has two feet, two hands and a family. Some people impress us as if they were relatively experienced human beings, having lived as men and women several times before. Once in a great while you meet someone who is really a master of living as a human being. He is really very experienced. But this life is only one life; this life is the human life. We cannot change all at once. Most of us have been born as human beings at least a few times. But we need more and more experience, more and more . . . .

Theravada Buddhism speaks about nirvana as being the final goal of this life, since human beings are full of pain and injustice. People should aspire to nirvana and say goodbye to human existence for good. Mahayana Buddhism has something different to say. Yes, life is full of egoism, full of contradiction, indeed full of pain and suffering. But, at the same time, life can be very happy and content. We can enjoy many wonderful encounters and experiences. We need something to study, to think about and to appreciate. Our life span is very short compared with the vastness of the universe and the complications of this world. We have a lot to learn and to master. So a Mahayana Buddhist says, "I should very much like to be born again as a human being." Positive thinking makes the positive possible. Negative thinking makes the negative possible.

Zazen is like dirt which you cannot detect. It is like the human dirt which attaches itself to your body. You yourself may not smell it, but someone else can. In Kyoto I have a good friend who sells incense. He continually smells of incense, but the scent has so penetrated into his body that he himself cannot smell it. In the same way, zazen also penetrates into your body and mind. When one eats, the food is digested and passes into the bloodstream. This process is called absorption. From the bloodstream the food passes into the cells. This is called assimilation. Zazen, too, gradually enters into our blood and into our cells. Above all, it enters into our inner Self. This cannot be accomplished instantly. Assimilation takes place gradually, but completely.

In this sense, zazen is like preparing water for tea. Usually we think that as long as the tea is hot, we have done a good job. This is true, of course, but there are two ways to make hot water. One way is to fill a kettle with lots of water and let it boil quickly over a high flame. Another way is to have the water come to a boil very slowly. Let it take an hour or so. Using the first method, the boiled water becomes cool after about fifteen minutes. But water that has been boiled slowly stays hot for a much longer period of time. It may seem strange, but I call this slow boiling, subtle boiling or cultivating the water. When the water is cultivated, the tea has a delicious taste. Attend one week-long sesshin and one week later zazen becomes cold. But zazen that is practiced day after day, month after month, sesshin after sesshin, year after year, even life after life, stays hot for a long time.

Still in all, we think that we are finite, and therefore we would like to get something out of zazen in a reasonable amount of time. Add patience and diligence! Today's koan is like Tozan's "Three Pounds of Flax":

> *Ummon was asked, "What is Buddha?"*
> *Ummon said, "A shit-stick!"*

In Japanese, Ummon's answer was *kan-shiketsu. Kan* means "dried"; *shiketsu* refers to some kind of tool made either of bamboo or wood which was used in China as a substitute for toilet paper. It was also used to carry dried dung from one place to another. We no longer find the kan-shiketsu in use in these modern days.

Now I have to remind you once again that there is no dogmatic Zen, no Zen theory and no Zen philosophy. There is only the constant realization of Self. Keeping our feet on the ground, there is only the constant revelation of THIS—as it is, at each moment. THIS is reality; THIS is no other than the manifestaion, the cause of Mu. So we say:

> *Buddha nature pervades the whole universe*
> *Revealing right here now . . . .*

Right here now, it is revealed as coughing, as a human being, as a drowsy state of mind. Right here now!

There is nothing in this world which is not the Buddha. To understand this we must particularly understand Ummon's "kan-shiketsu" or, as I translate it, "toilet paper." We must take care of the toilet paper which we use every day. We should treat it as if it were an intimate friend. But this attitude is, of course, not confined to toilet paper. We must become intimate with all things.

Someone who had been working on Ummon's "toilet paper" as a koan told me that now he cannot help but put his palms together in a gesture of reverence every time he uses toilet paper. This is what I call integration or penetration of the koan. And only when we have this can we say, "I understand this koan." Koan study should become part of everyday life. It is not particularly favorable to pass a koan quickly. It is better to struggle with it until we feel like offering incense to the toilet paper. Struggle until we can bow to a piece of toilet paper, instead of saying, "Ich!" or "Phooey!" Indeed, Zen is not a philosophy. It is a way of life.

To understand the significance of this koan, we must come to the point where we feel like bowing every time we carefully tear a sheet of paper from the roll. Take two or three sheets of paper and wipe. Wipe with single-minded care. Don't laugh! This is serious. If this attitude is not perfected, zazen loses its meaning.

The word, kan-shiketsu, came from Ummon's deep state of mind. With no whys or becauses, we can learn to appreciate kan-shiketsu with our own deep, deep breathing. If you understand this breath point, you can understand what Zen Buddhism is all about. What is Buddha? Toilet paper! That's all. What is this? Just breath after breath—JUST! THIS!

Some people think that it is enough if they are able to understand fundamental reality in terms of JUST-ness. It so happened that this week I broke a precious bowl. Fundamentally speaking, it is true that a broken bowl is JUST a broken bowl. But practically speaking, I should have been more careful. We have to learn how to incorporate the practical with the fundamental. We have to learn how to be careful, how to be productive, how to be sensible, how to be with it and, above all, how to be creative.

At the same time, we should have the constant awareness that things are as they are and cannot be otherwise. The statement: "Things are as they are and cannot be otherwise" itself gives a fatalistic and even nihilistic impression. But the plain fact is, right here, right now things are as they are and, indeed, cannot be otherwise. We just think and hope that they can be otherwise. Yet, things can be otherwise in the next moment if we cultivate a productive and creative attitude. Such an attitude can lead to many possible ways. We are walking on the endless path, yet each moment is the goal of the endless path. *Things are as they are and cannot be otherwise*!

"What is Buddha?"

"Toilet paper!"

Appreciate this dialogue!

New York Zendo Shobo-ji
February 13, 1977

Baso's Buddha Mind

The Gateless Gate: Case 30

The Koan:

> *Daibai once asked Baso, "What is Buddha?"*
> *Baso answered, "Mind is Buddha!"*

Mumon's Verse:

> *A fine day!*
> *The blue sky!*
> *Don't absent-mindedly look around*
> *Here and there.*
> *If you still ask, "What is Buddha?"*
> *It is like pocketing stolen goods*
> *And pleading innocent.*

The Teisho:

Today happens to be the Buddha's birthday and Good Friday; birth and death come together. Many people will be born today, and many people are passing away today—birth and death! To clarify what is birth and what is death is the most fundamental task of our practice. What is birth? What is death?

Buddha Shakyamuni was the son of a king of a small country located in what is now the southern part of Nepal. He was born five hundred sixty years before Christ in a garden called Lumbini, under a blossoming tree. His real name was Siddhartha Gautama. When he became a Buddha, that is, when he realized his Buddha nature and became the Enlightened One, he was called Buddha Shakyamuni. He lived eighty years and left a lasting influence upon his disciples. On the full-moon night of the second month, under a Sala tree, he passed away or, as we say, he entered *Parinirvana*. So he was born under a blossoming tree,

124

enlightened under the Bodhi tree and passed away under a Sala tree.

Maybe this is a good chance for us to clarify a few matters. We say, "Happy birthday!" but we never say, "Happy deathday!" We add various adjectives to describe certain occasions, such as "beautiful" wedding, "happy" anniversary, "tragic" death, etc. Now all of these are quite all right, but it is very important for us to see that there are two different ways of looking at reality: fundamentally and existentially. Fundamentally speaking, birth is just a phenomenon, to get married is another phenomenon, to get old is still another phenomenon, to get sick is a phenomenon and to die is a phenomenon. Just as I strike this lectern with my stick over and over again, fundamentally speaking, our lives are just a continuation of phenomenon, phenomenon, phenomenon. . . .

Existentially speaking, however, we do have preferences. We like something which is joyous, we dislike something which is sad. So we add all kinds of adjectives, such as beautiful, happy, great, fantastic, wonderful, etc., to describe our reactions. And all of these adjectives are derived from our existential point of view. This is quite all right. Happy birthday! Birthdays are happy! That is quite right. What is important for us to know is that there are these two aspects. The "happy" is from the existential point of view and "birth" is a fundamental phenomenon. Thus they are, of course, inseparable. We can say, "sad birthday," but we don't do so because birthdays are not sad. Most of our confusion comes because we consider the fundamental level (in Japanese honbun) and the existential level (in Japanese shusho) to be the same. We should see very plainly, the plain fact, the factuality that honbun and shusho, although they always appear simultaneously, must be distinguished from each other. If we had no emotions, it would be easy for us to understand everything. But then, life would be tasteless. Nevertheless it is these very emotions of ours that confuse us.

None of us prefer pain. But pain is nothing but pain!

Speaking about pain, I would like to tell you a story about a missionary who came to Japan and who developed stomach cancer. This missionary was suffering from incessant pain. Then, at one point, he felt that Jesus Christ on the Cross had endured pain, physically, mentally, emotionally, everything, much greater than his own. The missionary felt ashamed of his self-pitying attitude, so, knowing that he would die soon, he vowed that the last thing he would do in this world would be to receive all the pain from all suffering people. To his surprise he found that when he had rejected the pain, it had become excruciating. But when he actively welcomed it, his mind became more and more joyous. Each moment was bringing him a certain kind of satisfaction: at least he was absorbing someone else's pain and suffering.

He continued praying with all his might: "Pain, come to me pain, come on pain, okay pain, come pain, more, more. . . ." Still he felt that his suffering was not as great as that of Jesus Christ on the Cross, was not as painful as the Crucifixion. The days went by and not only did he not pass away, but he completely recovered.

This is a true story. I am not making it up just to encourage you. Now, it is interesting—how much does our mental attitude change things? What happens when we turn from hate to love, from rejection to reception?

During your zazen I trust that sometimes your pain is really excruciating. Try your best not to hate it. At least try to say, "All right, brothers and sisters, I will take all the pain from you." If you can truly say so, the hateful pain becomes a joyous pain. At the same time, you may go into a good condition for zazen.

Naturally we are egocentric, and when fragile samadhi comes, we strive to keep it. The very best way to increase the samadhi is to radiate it generously. Give! Radiate! Expand! Shine! It is in this way that gradually your inner door, so to speak, opens. This is the turning point from the ordinary way of thinking to the enlightened way of thinking. Sooner or later we have to take this attitude. The sooner we take it, the better. Our conventional way of thinking—that is, "I hate pain, I want to keep good zazen for myself"—doesn't work. This idea may seem crazy and revolutionary but, after all, enlightenment is spiritual revolution. Our conventional way of thinking has to be changed in order to deepen our zazen.

Now we often talk about deepening our zazen. In fact, we use the words "deep" and "profound" too much. What does "deep" mean? We know about deep breathing, but what about deep zazen? To do deep zazen refers to the breath. The breath almost stops, nothing is transferred somewhere else. Everything is right here, right now. Everything is clear. It is not necessary to push the breath, to regulate it or to be in hara. The breath goes all by itself. So natural! The mind is clear and transparent. It is as clear as the sky. We can often go into that kind of condition. That condition is what we call deep zazen.

When we are in deep zazen we feel that our center of gravity is set in our lower abdomen. This area that becomes the center of gravity is what we call hara, and when we find it, we experience a certain warmth and fulfillment of energy. This hara is the center of Zen practice. But for beginners, hara is difficult to feel, difficult to locate. Therefore some people, in their efforts to reach hara, put physical pressure on the area of their lower abdomen. This is wrong. Right now you are listening to my talk but you are not putting any physical pressure on your ears. You are seeing what is in front of you, but you are not putting physical pressure on your eyes. All you are doing is *paying attention*. By paying attention you hear and see better. In the same way, when you do zazen, just pay attention to your hara. There is no need for physical pressure.

There is a word in Latin, *spiritus*, which means "breath." The English word "spirit" derives from the Latin word spiritus. So, breath is spirit and spirit is no other than breath. During zazen, breathe carefully and naturally.

Daibai Hojo Zenji (751–839) asked, "What is Buddha?"

Don't look for the answer to this question in Buddhist metaphysics. Try to find some concrete response.

Baso Doitsu Zenji (709–88) said that Mind is Buddha. I say that breath is Buddha. So breathe in Buddha, hold Buddha and exhale Buddha!

Breath is the key to zazen. We know that we cannot speak without inhaling first and exhaling when our voices come out. Just before you jump, unconsciously you inhale. While you are jumping, you stop breathing. Once the jump is completed, you immediately exhale. Everybody does this even without being taught. The exhalation, the breathlessness, is more powerful than the inhalation.

It is the well-regulated breath that clears our minds and thus clarifies the Mind. In China and Japan, the character which represents the word "breath" consists of two parts: the top is the character for "self" and the bottom is the character for "mind." So Self-Mind is no other than breath and breath is no other than Self-Mind. Breath is no other than Buddha. While you are inhaling and exhaling:

> *Don't absent-mindedly look around*
> *Here and there*

asking what is Buddha!

> *If you still ask, "What is Buddha?"*

after inhaling it and holding it in your hara "pocket," you are

> *. . . pocketing the stolen goods*
> *And pleading innocent.*

Dai Bosatsu Zendo Kongo-ji
April 8, 1977

Ummon's Off the Track

The Gateless Gate: Case 39

The Koan:

A monk began a question to Ummon by reciting this verse: "The light serenely shines throughout the whole universe—"
Ummon suddenly interrupted him. "Isn't this Choseisu's poem?"
The monk said, "Yes, it is."
Ummon said, "You're off the track!"
Later Shishin gave a talk on this koan and asked his students, "Tell me, how did this monk miss it?"

The Teisho:

Today is a story about Ummon Bun'en Zenji. I have already introduced you to this extremely outstanding Zen master. However, before we go into the koan itself, let us think about something.

Now, in general, it is said that there are two Zen schools: Rinzai and Soto. We know that during the T'ang Dynasty there were five Zen schools: Rinzai, Soto, Ummon, Igyo and Hogen. But we also know that during that time there were great masters such as Nansen, Joshu, Hyakujo, Tokusan, and many others. You may wonder, "If there is a Rinzai School, why not a Tokusan School or a Joshu School?" Now let us think. This kind of thinking is good because we are not indulging in just miscellaneous, fanciful thoughts. When we appreciate Ummon's koan, we can almost immediately tell that this is Ummon since it has a certain characteristic. The same is true of many other teachers. So Ummon's Zen was created by venerable Ummon Bun'en; Rinzai's Zen was created by venerable Rinzai Gigen; Hakuin's Zen was created by venerable Hakuin Ekaku. Since our sangha follows one of the lineages that has descended from the Rinzai School, every evening we recite the "Teidai Dempo" (the "Names of the Patriarchs") in which appears "Hakuin Ekaku Zenji Dai Osho." But Hakuin's Zen and Rinzai's Zen are quite different, as different as venerable Rinzai Gigen was from venerable Hakuin Ekaku. Gempo Roshi's Zen is different from Rinzai's Zen. Soen Roshi's Zen is different from Hakuin's Zen. Yasutani Roshi's Zen is also unique. So all are different. And your Zen is different too.

In other words, everybody here eats the same food, that is, everybody here does zazen. But our stomachs vary, our way of digesting the food varies, our way of producing energy varies, and, therefore, our different personalities are born. It should be so. If we were all the same, we would be not at all interesting.

The great teachers were very creative. There were no men like Ummon before Ummon. No one can really imitate Ummon. So Ummon had his own world which was created by him. And that unique creativity made Ummon great.

There are many different degrees of creativity. Let's look at artists, for example. In my opinion, the *real* artist is the one who has created his own unique world of expression. And no one can imitate it. Most of you may consider Picasso one of the greatest artists in the twentieth century simply because he created his own world. The same is true of Chagall. Chagall has his own world. The moment we see one of his paintings we know it's Chagall. I may also mention these artists: Beethoven, Bach, Mozart, Shakespeare and Dostoevski—all of whom will be remembered throughout history.

Zazen is a practice of creativity. It creates unique personalities who then create their own styles, as it were. Sitting, sitting, sitting . . . . As a result of this sitting, without intending to create anything in particular, each person's unique nature is revealed. We often say, "There are so many characters in the zendo!" Maybe, from the start, characters are attracted to Zen. Surprisingly, however, because of Zen practice, not only does a character take on character, but he also becomes even more of a character himself.

In order to learn something we have to receive guidance and instruction from a teacher. And that is why, when I give this kind of talk, the influences of both Soen Roshi and Yasutani Roshi are undeniable. As my teachers, they provided me with real nourishment. I cannot imitate

Soen Roshi's Zen, nor can I imitate Yasutani Roshi's Zen. Yet my Zen was a result of the influence of my teachers, combined with years of zazen practice. With continuous zazen and with continuous creativity, I hope that it will grow.

So, strictly speaking, there is no such thing as the Rinzai School of Zen or the Soto School of Zen. But there is Rinzai's Zen, Sozan's Zen, Tosan's Zen and Dogen's Zen. Each one is unique and should be so.

But why today are there only two practicing schools of Zen? Ummon's school, for instance, disappeared because his Zen was too unique for anyone to succeed it. And other schools have disappeared simply for lack of Dharma successors.

So let's go into today's koan: A traveling monk once wanted to ask Master Ummon a question. But instead of just stating a question, he started to recite a short verse:

> The light serenely shines throughout the
> whole universe—

And the next line goes:

> The ignorant and the wise live together.

But even before this monk had a chance to finish the first line, Ummon interrupted, "Just a second. Isn't that Chosetsu's poem?"

For the monk this was an unexpected interruption. So he said, "Oh, yes."

Then Ummon said, "You're off the track!"

Another way to translate Ummon's response is: "You have missed it!"

During the morning service we begin the dedication by reciting:

> Buddha nature pervades the whole universe,
> Revealing right here now.

This line is very much like: "The light serenely shines throughout the whole universe." Now suppose one of you wanted to ask me a question and you began to speak by reciting: "Buddha nature pervades the whole universe, revealing right here now . . ." Interrupting you, I would ask, "Isn't that from the morning service dedication?" Most of you would honestly say, "Yes, it is." And I would have to say, "You're off the track!"

Why? First, this recitation is not your own creative expression. Second, because it is not your own, what you are saying is not as real as what you have experienced. If you are speaking from your own experience, no one can interrupt your flow of words. Thus you can never be off the track. You make your own track as you go.

A Chinese saying goes:

> *That which enters from the outside, can*
> *never become your own real treasure.*

However lofty and poetic your words may be, so long as they are not your own creative expression, you are off the track. And so long as you repeat something which has already been said, you are leaving an unnecessary trace.

> *The moonlight penetrates into the*
> *bottom of the pool,*
> *Yet no trace is left.*

Moonlight is the moon's original expression. Hence, not a trace is left. But the above verse itself has already left a trace. However truthful it may be, it is not direct expression. It is unnecessary for the moon to say: "My light leaves no trace." But human beings want to describe it, even though the description weakens the impact. It's better to say nothing at all.

There is a very well-known haiku by Chiyojo which goes:

> *Morning-glory!*
> *Growing 'round the well rope.*
> *I get water elsewhere.*

This is a beautiful haiku expressing the compassion of the poetess. However, if Chiyojo had not added the last line, this haiku would have been even better. And yet I presume that it is the last line that she wanted to emphasize the most. The morning-glory, just like the moonlight, was doing its own thing—blooming. But Chiyojo's so-called compassionate nature, that is, "I don't want to break the morning-glory's vine, so I will make a special effort to get water from another place," is off the track. It leaves a trace.

A similar example is found in *The Blue Rock Collection*. Chokei and Hofuku were traveling together. The younger Dharma brother, Hofuku, had recently realized that "Buddha nature pervades the whole universe, revealing right here, right now." So he was feeling very elated. When the two monks reached the top of a mountain, with great joy, Hofuku, stamping his feet on the ground, said to his elder Dharma brother, "Isn't this reality, too?"

Chokei said, "Yes, it is. But it's a pity to say so."

This "it's a pity to say so" has deep meaning. It's a pity that Chiyojo had to say, "I get water elsewhere." And it's a pity to say, "Yet no trace is left." And certainly, it's a pity to give this kind of talk.

> *Buddha nature pervades the whole*
> *universe,*
> *Revealing right here now.*

This is true. Buddha nature does pervade and is revealed. But some of us may think that Buddha nature is always something good, and therefore it's supposed to be something joyous and positive. We ignore, in fact intentionally ignore, the fact that Buddha nature can sometimes be painful. So long as Buddha nature *pervades* the whole universe, it must have both negative and positive aspects—like day and night. The true Buddha nature, which reveals itself right here, right now, refuses to abide by our preferences. So strictly speaking, whether we count our breath or not, whether we do Mu or not, whether we do shikantaza or not, whether we attend sesshin or not, even prior to the creation of heaven and earth and even after the deterioration of heaven and earth, "Buddha nature pervades the whole universe, revealing right here, right now." If this is truly understood throughout your total being, you don't have to count your breath, you don't have to attend a sesshin. You can just take it easy! But since, so far, we have not pacified our minds to that extent, we do count our breath, we do attend sesshin, we do work on Mu, and we do have to recite each morning:

> The Dharma,
> Incomparably profound and minutely subtle,
> Is hardly met with
> Even in hundreds of thousands of millions
>   of eons,
> We now can see it,
> Listen to it,
> Accept and hold it;
> May we completely understand and actualize
> The Tathagata's true meaning.

The true meaning of the Tathagata is no other than:

> Buddha nature pervades the whole
>   universe,
> Revealing right here now.

Dai Bosatsu Zendo Kongo-ji
September 5, 1977

Daitsu Chisho Buddha

The Gateless Gate: Case 9

The Koan:

A monk asked Master Seijo, "Daitsu Chisho Buddha did zazen for ten kalpas. Still Buddha-Dharma was not manifested, nor did he attain Buddhahood. Why?"

Seijo said, "Oh, that's a wonderful question!"

The monk persisted, "He did zazen for such a long time. Why did he not attain Buddhahood?"

Seijo replied, "Because he cannot become Buddha."

The Teisho:

Today is Sunday, November 14, 1976.

From time to time I begin my teisho by saying, "Today is such and such a day, such and such a month and year." Some of you may think that I am reminding you of the date for your information or because the talk is being recorded. Of course in one sense this is true, but as long as we are talking about THIS matter—TODAY IS SUNDAY, NOVEMBER 14, 1976! Whether we like the number 14 or not, whether this is someone's birthday or not, whether we like Sunday or not—TODAY IS SUNDAY, NOVEMBER THE FOURTEENTH and cannot be otherwise! This expression is very important—*cannot be otherwise*. Today is the 14th, yesterday was the 13th and tomorrow will be the 15th. It is easy to accept this. We have no complaints, no objections. When it comes to some other matter, however, even though we know it *cannot be otherwise*, we delude ourselves by thinking that it can be otherwise. This gap between the fact of it cannot-be-otherwise and the hope that it can-be-otherwise is what brings us all sorts of negative feelings, such as frustration, anxiety and dissatisfaction. If we were only able to accept everything that happens as nicely as we accept the fact that today is November 14, 1976, without fail, our minds would be at peace. And this "mind at peace" is exactly what we are seeking.

Right now, everything is all right. If we were able to continue this present state of well-being, and if we were able to stabilize it, then it would be possible to accept all things—the good and the bad. But at times we have doubts about tomorrow, and at times we are suspicious about the day after tomorrow. Challenging our doubts and suspicions, we do zazen practice. And overcome them.

Zazen practice is the practice of changing our attitude toward all things which confront us in our everyday lives. That is, to attain "the mind at peace" no matter what happens and to share it with others is exactly what zazen practice is all about.

Some people think that to do zazen at home by oneself is better than sitting with the sangha. Others think that sangha togetherness is better than sitting alone. Each helps the other. There is a European coin that has the words "alone very well" engraved upon it. If you don't understand this motto, make it your koan. American coins say, "In God we trust." But "alone very well . . . ," "all one very well . . ."

In any case, today's koan is Daitsu Chisho. This Buddha did zazen for ten kalpas. Let me explain to you how long one kalpa is. Consider a rock which is forty square miles across and forty square miles up and down. Once every one hundred years, a beautiful angel comes down from heaven wearing a silk robe. As she dances on the rock, her robe sweeps it surface. After her dance she returns to heaven. Again, after another century has elapsed, in her silk robe she repeats the same dance on the rock. The time it takes for her to wear down that entire rock, so that nothing is left, is called one kalpa. There is another way of calculating the length of time of one kalpa. A container, forty miles high and forty miles wide, is filled with poppy seeds. Once every one hundred years, a heavenly being comes down and takes one poppy seed. When all of the poppy seeds are taken, that length of time is called one kalpa.

So this Daitsu Chisho Buddha did zazen for ten kalpas, such a long, long time, and, nevertheless, did not attain Buddhahood. Why? This is the question. Some of you complain, "I have been doing zazen for about three months and I haven't felt a thing," or "I have been doing Mu for half a year, still I don't know what Mu is." Daitsu Chisho

Buddha is said to have sat for ten kalpas. Now, it is at this point that we have to switch our minds from the ordinary to the extraordinary way of thinking. The ordinary way of thinking makes us ask, "How long does it take to get attainment?" or "Because I do this, will I get that?" What I mean by "extraordinary way of thinking" is like what Master Hakuin said in *The Song of Zazen*:

All beings are primarily Buddhas.

Now, how can the Buddha become more Buddha?

Some of you may say, "If this is true, I will go out and enjoy the sunshine because I am already Buddha and I cannot become more Buddha." But I am sure that you will not do so. Why? Just to say that "all beings are primarily Buddhas" doesn't help. Such statements do not give us "the mind at peace."

There are two kinds of enlightenment. One is called *honrai jobutsu*, which means "we are all fundamentally enlightened." The second is *kensho jobutsu*, which means "the existential experience of enlightenment." I will give you an example. Suppose there is a person. Fundamentally, whether he is in a good mood or not, that person is still that person and cannot be otherwise. But he can become a monk, or a doctor or a fireman. He can become anything—a better person, a more understanding person, a more sympathetic person. So existentially he can become endlessly better, but fundamentally he is himself. What we are involved with here in this zendo is to realize that fundamentally we are Buddha and cannot be otherwise. And, at the same time, existentially we can become more mindful, more patient, more calm, etc. The fundamental truth is the truth, but it is also like the menu in a restaurant. It lists all the food but it doesn't fill our stomachs.

So, fundamentally speaking, we cannot become more Buddha, but existentially speaking, we can become a better Buddha. It is very important for us to clearly distinguish between the two. When you are asked to give a lecture on Zen Buddhism, the first thing you should explain is honbun and shusho, that is, fundamental reality and existential or phenomenological reality. Unless the distinction between these two is clearly explained, confusion will not be resolved. When honbun and shusho are well understood, all the koans will make absolutely perfect sense.

Metaphorically, honbun and shusho may be explained like this: fundamentally, the ocean is the ocean, but phenomenologically, there are many waves. Some of these waves are turbulent and some are just ripples. Fundamentally, we are like the Pacific Ocean. The Pacific Ocean cannot be more Pacific. All the same, the condition of our waves changes. They are sometimes polluted, sometimes stormy and sometimes peaceful. But these two, ocean and wave—fundamental and existential—can never, not even for one second, be separated from each other.

Consider Daitsu Chisho Buddha as the Pacific Ocean. Even after ten kalpas of being, the Pacific Ocean is still an ocean and cannot become more ocean. If this is "pacifically" understood, then our minds will be pacified.

Dai Bosatsu Zendo Kongo-ji
November 14, 1976

Echu's Three Calls

The Gateless Gate: Case 17

The Koan:

    Echu Kokushi, the emperor's teacher, called to his attendant, "Oshin!"
    Oshin answered, "Hai!" (Yes!)
    Echu repeated, "Oshin!"
    "Hai!"
    Once more, "Oshin!"
    "Hai!"
    Echu said, "I have been thinking that I am independent, but now I realize that you, too, are an independent fellow."

The Teisho:

There are many translations for this koan but as long as we argue over words and names, no matter how musical or excellent they may be, we will not reach the main point. After all, koans were written in ancient Chinese, which is even more difficult to understand and translate into modern English than Japanese. Our practice, as the saying goes, "not depending upon words and names, directly points to the Nature of man."

The two characters who appear in today's story are Nanyo Echu Kokushi (d. 776) and his student, Oshin Tangen Zenji. The honorific title *kokushi*, by the way, means "national teacher." It is not particularly necessary to ascertain when this dialogue took place. It could have occurred when Oshin had just come to study with Echu. Or, it could have taken place after Oshin had spent years and years of practice with Echu. Most likely the latter was the case.

Before I go into today's case, let me tell you another story involving these two men. This story is from *The Blue Rock Collection*.

When Master Echu had become very old, the emperor came to see him. "After your death, is there anything that I can do for you?"

The National Teacher replied, "Erect a seamless tombstone for me!"

The emperor then asked, "Please tell me what you mean by a 'seamless tombstone.'"

The National Teacher sat in zazen in front of the emperor revealing his True Nature. "Do you understand?"

"No, I don't."

"I have a Dharma successor, Oshin Tangen, who knows the real meaning of 'seamless tombstone.' Ask him."

When the teacher passed away, the emperor met with Oshin. "Our teacher told me that he would like to have a seamless tombstone erected. Do you know what this means?"

To this question, Oshin Tangen replied in verse:

> South of the lake, north of the river,
> There is a country filled with gold.
> Under the shadowless trees, there is a ferry boat.
> When all the passengers reach their destination,
> They no longer know each other.

In the Sangha Meadow, our cemetery at Dai Bosatsu Zendo, there is a wooden commemorative post, called *toba* in Japanese. On this toba I have written Oshin's verse. There, under "the shadowless trees" and shapeless tombstones, the sangha ferry has brought the ashes of our deceased Dharma brothers and sisters. At last, race-less, age-less, sex-less sangha togetherness!

In any case, Oshin Tangen was Echu's attendant monk. One day, the following dialogue took place:

"Oshin!"

"Hai!"

"Oshin!"

"Hai!"

"Oshin!"

"Hai!"

Now Echu called Oshin three times. Normally, it is enough to call somebody only once. And normally, when someone is called, he responds, "Yes? Did you call me?" or "Yes? May I help you?" or "Yes? What is it?" After being attendant to this National Teacher for many years, Oshin was aware of the fact that Echu was not calling for help with some everyday matter. Oshin understood that Echu's calls were expressions of what could be termed "this fundamental matter."

"Oshin!"
"Hai!"
"Oshin"
"Hai!"
"Oshin!"
"Hai!"

Between the call and the response—no more, no less and no-thing! No need to call three times! Once is enough: "OSHIN!" "HAI!" It is not even necessary to call or to answer. This fundamental matter is unnameable:

> There is a reality even prior to heaven and earth;
> Indeed, it has no form, much less a name.

Now the problem is that normally we feel that the so-called practical life is everything. But this is only half of the truth. In our practical life we say, "Yes? May I help you?" or "Yes? Did you call me?" or "Yes? What can I do for you?" All of these are important statements. At the same time, when we look at the dialogue between Echu and Oshin from the fundamental point of view, Oshin's "Yes!" is the perfect manifestation of his Buddha nature—revealed. There is nothing esoteric, nothing concealed. "Yes!" is very natural, and yet it is perfect revelation. Most of us have not yet realized this manifestation and therefore think that Oshin's "Yes!" is just a simple affirmation. Some may even think that both Echu and Oshin are either deaf or stupid.

There is no need to particularly say, "Yes!" "Yeah" is all right, too. In fact, silence even is better. So whether someone answers "Yes!" in a loud voice or a soft voice, whether someone answers in Japanese "Hai!" or in American slang "Yeah!" doesn't matter. They are all fundamentally the same; they are all manifestations of Buddha nature.

I am afraid that these statements may give you the wrong impression.

You may get the idea that it is all right to behave in any fashion, according to your mood, as long as everything is nothing but the manifestation of Buddha nature. But you are only fifty percent right. Remember that if you behave respectfully, you will be respected in return. If you speak single-mindedly, you will leave a better impression. At New York Zendo, the telephone is almost constantly ringing, for many people call for information. What kind of impression will people receive if you answer the telephone saying, "Yes, may I help you?" or "Watcha want?" Somehow we must learn to balance the "freedom" of fundamental reality with the "etiquette" of existential reality. Although variety appears in existential, pragmatic reality, our words, conveyed by our breath, are nothing but the blossoms of Buddha nature. With zazen practice we can understand that all phenomena, even the emotional and psychological phenomena of preferences, which are the cause of suffering, are Buddha nature itself.

The outside world cannot be changed. But our minds, our attitudes, our preferences and our ways of looking at the outside world can be changed. Effort, introspection and clarity, applied with the BREATH, do change our way of looking at things. And this changing is no other than the Zen realization, through which our lives become richer and more filled with gratefulness and appreciation.

Echu said, "I have been thinking that I am independent, but now I realize that you, too, are an independent fellow."

Legend says that when Shakyamuni Buddha was born under a blossoming tree, he stood up, walked seven steps towards each of the four directions, held his right hand up, pointing to the heavens, and his left hand down, pointing to the earth, and said:

Above Heaven, below Earth, I alone am the World Honored One.

So not only is Shakyamuni Buddha the World Honored One, but also the National Teacher, his student, Oshin, and all of us are alone the World Honored One. In other words, we are completely independent, we are as we are, right here, right now, and we cannot be otherwise! A famous poem concerning Echu's three calls and Oshin's three responses goes:

A mirror reflects the candlelight in the golden palace.
A mountain echoes the temple bell in the moonlight.

Each reflection is as independent as Echu's call and Oshin's response.
Each echo is as independent as Echu's call and Oshin's response.

New York Zendo Shobo-ji
January 18, 1977

Tokusan and Isan

The Blue Rock Collection: Case 4

The Koan:

> Tokusan came to Isan's temple, a pilgrim's bundle flung over his shoulder. He went straight up to the Dharma Hall. Walking from east to west and west to east, he looked around and said, "Nothing! Nothing!"
> Then he left.
> Reaching the gate, he reflected, "I must not be so abrupt. I must not be too hasty."
> Preparing himself in the proper way, Tokusan reentered the monastery, this time formally announcing his visit.
> When Isan was seated, Tokusan solemnly spread out his kneeling cloth and said, "Master!"
> Isan made an action as if to reach for his ceremonial whisk. Whereupon Tokusan shouted and shook his sleeves. Turning his back on the Dharma Hall, Tokusan put on his straw sandals and went on his way.
> In the evening Isan asked the head monk, "Where is the newcomer who came here today?"
> The head monk answered, "Turning his back on the Dharma Hall, he put on his sandals and left."
> Isan then said, "You will see that some day this noble young man is going to build a straw hut on the highest mountain peak and slander the Buddha and abuse the patriarchs."

The Teisho:

Today I will start by reading a letter which I have just received from Sister Jeannine, a Catholic nun who comes to sit regularly at New York Zendo.

Dear Eido Roshi,

This letter gives me the opportunity to let you know how I am getting along with my meditation, with my zazen. As I already told you last week, since my last sesshin, I think that I can say that it is going all right. Nothing extraordinary has happened. On the contrary, I have been experiencing a continual quiet, peaceful joy and very often a kind of "oneness." Occasionally there is disharmony or annoyance, but it quickly changes into deeper awareness.

There were things in my own religion that I firmly believed in, but that I could not understand. I used to wonder how some things could be possible. But ever since the last sesshin, I now think that I am beginning to understand.

The last day of the sesshin and all night long were passed in meditation. It was a wonderful, indeed a very wonderful experience. My mind was completely quiet, empty, just repeating "Jesus," with no thought of myself. Just being—unification with one and all. Once, after the sesshin, while the priest was saying Mass, I experienced a similar oneness. Most of the time it is very soft and wonderful.

When one wants to talk of an experience, words are certainly in the way. Maybe it would be helpful to you if I tell of my experience according to what I believe to be in my own Christianity. I do not pretend that I have it all. I am so little. It is only my own small description.

This emptying of the mind, this union, this oneness that I experienced that night is what I think is called "the presence of God," "complete union with God," "at one with God." When I really experienced the presence of God in my life, there was absolutely no thought, no images, no words at all. It was just complete silence, at one with all, completely aware, completely mindful of each moment and action. These moments were short compared to the length of time of the sesshin. As I go deeper with Mu, it is also what we call "the presence of God."

When I first came to the zendo, someone said, "Let's put ourselves together," or something like that. I felt as if I knew what was meant. I was very comfortable with this expression. Just the same, I used to ask myself, "How can I put it into my own religion?" One day it came to me. When starting our prayers we say, "Let us place ourselves in the presence of God and adore Him profoundly." They were just words, but for me they represented an attitude of being. It is the same as St. Paul writes: "I live, no not I, but Christ lives in me." Also in the Bible it is written: "I sleep but my heart is awake."

I have written all this, but I think that it is just words. You must think the same. Pardon me for so many words. Please forget about them. How can I compare an experience with words! So, I had better stop.

I hope that you have another wonderful sesshin. Also, wishing you a safe trip to Japan and thank you for your kind help.

Jeannine

I have read this letter with the hope that it may become an inspiration for your zazen. Indeed, everyone, whether they are a Catholic nun or whoever they may be, can experience the taste of zazen. And as Sister Jeannine said, her understanding of Christianity became much clearer through her own sitting. It should be so.

Today's koan: Tokusan came to Isan's temple. If some of you are not familiar with this kind of Zen Buddhist teisho, you may wonder about the relationship between Tokusan and Isan. Their actions appear almost incomprehensible. What is the connection between Mu practice and deep samadhi? Or, what is the connection between unification with the presence of God and this Dharma battle between Tokusan and Isan? To answer these questions, let me say a few words before we go into the koan itself.

The central theme of the practice of zazen is to become aware of the plain factuality of the universe. The plain factuality of the universe is that heaven, earth and Self are one. This is not a theory. This is a fact. And about this fact, which we are trying to experience little by little, there is actually nothing to say, nothing to ask. There is no coming, no going. There is no self to be called the subject and no other to be called the object. The plain factuality of the universe is that trees are all right as trees, stones are okay as stones, broken tea bowls are broken tea bowls and cannot be otherwise. Take for instance the noise of the vacuum cleaner and the sound of the gong. We prefer the sound of the gong. But both the noise of the vacuum cleaner and the sound of the gong are phenomena and cannot be otherwise. At this moment, whether we like them or not, things, both pleasant and annoying, are nothing but phenomena. We have no other choice but to accept them as they are.

To understand this factuality, not just through your mind, but through your total being, is the purpose of zazen practice. Today's koan and all Zen stories may seem very strange and sometimes they may even seem crazy. But by understanding cultural and linguistic differences, and by deepening our zazen, and by learning to think with hara instead of with the brain, these stories begin to make sense. They are all simply pointing to one phenomenon after another. It is like sesshin when the second day of zazen is better than the first day, the fourth day of zazen becomes more clear than the third day and the sixth day is better than the fifth day. In such a way, we begin to understand that heaven and earth and Self are, after all, one matter, and that one matter is the very matter for which we are striving. Keeping this introduction in your mind, the story of Tokusan and Isan can be more readily appreciated.

Now to begin with, I should like to introduce the two masters, Tokusan Senkan Zenji (780/2–865) and Isan Reiyu Zenji (771–853).

One day Tokusan stopped at a tea house for some refreshment. Since he was a scholar of the *Diamond Sutra*, he was carrying a copy of it along with many books of commentaries. The old woman who ran the tea house, noticing what Tokusan was carrying, said to him, "What do you have with you?"

Tokusan proudly said, "These are profound books concerning the teachings of the *Diamond Sutra*. I am hungry. May I have something to eat?"

Then the old woman said, "Wait a second! If you can answer my question, I will be happy to bring you something to eat, free of charge."

Tokusan said, "Go ahead! Ask anything!"

So she said, "In the *Diamond Sutra* there is a phrase which goes: 'Past mind cannot be grasped, present mind cannot be grasped, future mind cannot be grasped.' You told me that you would like to have a snack. Now tell me, with which mind will you appreciate the food?"

Tokusan was dumbfounded and could not answer. He thought that this must be an extraordinary woman. This time he humbly asked her who her teacher was. She told him that her teacher was Master Ryutan and suggested that Tokusan visit him.

When Tokusan met with Master Ryutan, they spent most of the evening discussing the *Diamond Sutra* and Zen Buddhism. Finally they decided to retire. Since it was dark outside, Ryutan gave Tokusan a candle to light his way. Just when Tokusan took it, Ryutan blew out the flame. All was dark! At this very moment Tokusan transcended his intellectual interpretations of the *Diamond Sutra*.

On the following day Tokusan burned his copy of the *Diamond Sutra*. And it is that burnt *Diamond Sutra* which is, even today, helping our zazen tremendously.

About Isan: when he was a young monk he was at Hyakujo's monastery as the tenzo. An outsider, who had some kind of psychic ability, had found a mountain which he thought would be a wonderful place for a monastery. He told Hyakujo that the mountain had a certain atmosphere and if a monastery were to be built there, fifteen hundred monks would eventually live and practice in it. Hyakujo himself was very interested, but the psychic said, "No, you cannot go. Your face is not rich enough."

So in order to find someone to found that monastery, Hyakujo decided to test his chief disciples. One day he placed a pitcher on the ground. He first asked the head monk, "If you do not call this a pitcher, what do you call it?"

The head monk replied, "I cannot call it a wooden shoe."

Then Hyakujo asked Isan the same question. Isan kicked the pitcher and walked away. Hyakujo then announced that the head monk was defeated by the tenzo monk. Thus Isan was sent to the mountain to establish the new monastery.

At that time, Isan was not yet called Isan, since Isan was actually the name of the mountain. Because the monastery was not yet built when Isan arrived on the mountain, he just sat. The story goes that animals brought him nuts and other food to eat. Isan just continued to sit, with no friends and no sangha. After seven years, even this very patient monk started to have doubts. Finally he decided to give up. On the very day that he was to leave, a tiger came and tugged on his sleeve as though it were telling him to stay. This made Isan change his mind and he stayed. A few days later, a traveling monk appeared. Now there were two. Once there were two, there was already a sangha. If there is just one person there is no sangha—sangha is plural. Isan and this traveling monk established a sangha, and eventually another monk appeared. Thus, gradually, the sangha became larger and larger. The monastery was built and it is said that fifteen hundred monks did gather there. Now the Chinese tend toward exaggeration, but perhaps in this case there was no exaggeration. Indeed, many monks lived together.

So, getting back to the koan . . . one day Tokusan appeared at Isan's monastery. Tokusan and Isan! Isan was much older than Tokusan and was much more mature.

Tokusan was visiting various Zen masters, as was the custom of the time. He arrived at Isan's temple with his bag informally flung over his shoulder. The formal way of carrying the pilgrim's bag is to suspend it from the neck so that it hangs over the chest. So before anything happens, we can notice something of Tokusan's attitude. Without even a greeting, he just entered the Dharma Hall, walked from east to west and west to east and said, "Nothing! Nothing!"

Rules of etiquette, morality and ethics are just patterns of behavior established by human beings. To be polite is considered better than being rude. But this is a judgment that we make according to our own preferences, according to our existential viewpoint of reality. When seen in this way, Tokusan's manner appears to be very rude. Actually, when Tokusan walked from east to west and looked around, he was expressing his true understanding; that is, there is nothing, not a thing which is superfluous, not a thing which is deficient. No coming, no going; no east, no west.

At the gate Tokusan stopped to reflect, "I must not be so abrupt. I must be more gentle."

Here is Tokusan's dilemma. Because of years of habit, living in the world of human beings, Tokusan does know what is polite and what is rude. He knows that these rules are extremely important as a means of preserving harmony in human society. Social conventions are deeply rooted in his mind: to be polite is good, to be rude is bad. At the same time, Tokusan also knows the plain factuality: there is "nothing" to be called polite and "nothing" to be called rude.

So, preparing himself in the proper way, Tokusan re-entered the monastery, this time formally announcing his visit. Tokusan is abiding by the rules of existential, everyday human reality.

When Isan was seated, Tokusan solemnly spread out his kneeling cloth and said, "Master!" This "Master!" was Tokusan's expression of true understanding.

Upon receiving this "true" greeting, Isan responded accordingly. He reached for his ceremonial whisk, intending to strike Tokusan. Tokusan echoed Isan's action by shouting and waving his sleeves, again transcending the customary rules of etiquette. We, on the other hand, are normally trapped by these rules.

Isan must have been very impressed with Tokusan's spontaneous actions. With great admiration he later told his head monk, "You will see that some day this noble young man is going to build a straw hut on the highest mountain peak and slander the Buddha and abuse the patriarchs."

When you hear such expressions as "straw hut" and "mountain peak," you may wonder whether Zen Buddhism is aiming for escape or alienation from society. When you hear such words as "slander" and "abuse," you may wonder whether Zen Buddhism is full of violence. Let us remember that these expressions are translated from ancient Chinese, and it is very difficult to render the ancient Chinese way of thinking into direct, concise, modern English. Actually, these expressions refer to Tokusan's freedom—freedom to build a hut, freedom to go to the top of a mountain, without hesitating, and freedom to abuse or praise, as he wishes. In other words, Isan's statement reveals nothing but his highest esteem for Tokusan, a man of freedom.

Dai Bosatsu Zendo Kongo-ji
October 14, 1975

Nansen's Path

The Gateless Gate : Case 19

The Koan:

> *Joshu asked Nansen, "What is the Path?"*
> *Nansen replied, "Everyday life is the Path."*
> *Joshu: "Can it be mastered?"*
> *Nansen: "The more you try to master it, the more it will evade you."*
> *Joshu: "If I do not try to master the Tao, how can I know it is the Path?"*
> *Nansen: "The Path does not belong to the world of senses. Neither does it belong to a world absent of senses. Knowledge is a delusion and ignorance is senseless. If you want to attain the True Path, make yourself as vast and free as the sky. Name it neither good nor not good as you like."*
> *With these words, Joshu was enlightened.*

Mumon's Comment:

> *Nansen should have resolved Joshu's doubts as soon as Joshu asked the questions. I don't believe that Joshu understood what Nansen meant. He needed at least thirty more years of practice.*

The Verse:

> *In spring, hundreds of flowers;*
> *In autumn, a clear full moon;*
> *In summer, a cool breeze;*
> *In winter, snowflakes:*
> *With no hang-ups in your mind,*
> *Every season is a good season!*

The Teisho:

Today is the sixth day of Rohatsu Sesshin. Only tonight and tomorrow is left. Even though we are a little tired, our minds are clear. Therefore we can clearly see, clearly smell, clearly taste. We are content. Tomorrow night we will sit until midnight, and the following morning we will commemorate the Buddha's enlightenment. In fact, we will be commemorating, celebrating and congratulating ourselves on our own insight.

So today: Nansen Fugan Zenji (748–835) and Joshu Jushin Zenji (778–897) are appearing together in a very famous koan. Joshu asked Nansen, "What is the Path?" The "Path" that appears in this question is the English translation of the Chinese word *tao*. In Japanese it is pronounced *dō*.

Buddhism itself originated in India and many terms which we use, such as *Buddha, dharma, dhyana, nirvana, prajna, samadhi* and *sunyata* are Sanskrit words. When Buddhism moved from India to China, translations of the Buddhist texts were naturally needed. Some words, however, were not translated. Rather, they were transliterated. For example, the word *bodhisattva* was first written in Chinese *bodaisatta*. Then it was finally abbreviated to *bosatsu*. Other words such as nirvana and sunyata were translated. The translators chose to represent sunyata with the Chinese character that represents "sky" and "emptiness." Sky is not an entity unto itself. It has no contained existence. Although we say that the sky is either sunny, cloudy, rainy, etc., actually the sky itself is empty. So "sky" and "emptiness' is a beautiful translation of sunyata.

The Indian mentality is highly metaphysical and speculative, while the Chinese mentality has its two feet on the ground. So when the Chinese scholars were translating the metaphysical ideas of the Indian Buddhist philosophers, they had to find some equivalent Chinese words. One of these words was *tao*. As Taoism was already established, the word tao was familiar to the Chinese in their everyday lives. Both the idea of Tao and the word "tao" itself were deeply rooted in the Chinese mind. Metaphysically, Tao means Ultimate Reality, or Way. Concretely, tao means way or path. Now when this double-meaning word Tao came to Japan, it was pronounced *dō*.

Etymologically speaking, Tao means the pathway which allows people to reach their destination. However, keep in mind that when you reach your destination, you should still continue. When you accomplish something, you should not become attached to it. Be free from Tao. But in order to reach something, we have to follow a way and we have to walk on the path with our own efforts. The path, therefore, shows us the direction which we follow. Thus we reach the Path.

In the Japanese culture there are many "Ways." For example, the art of calligraphy is called *Shodo*. *Sho* means "writing" and "calligraphy," and *do* is "way." From the Japanese point of view, calligraphy is not just an art. Rather it is itself a Way or a way to reach the Way. With the posture of zazen, we make the ink. With the regulated breath, we write, write, and write. This is one kind of concentration practice. It is also an aesthetic and a practical practice. By following the Way of Calligraphy, one meets a certain spirituality.

Kendo is another such practice. Not only does the student of Kendo learn how to use the sword skillfully, but he also is subject to strict discipline and training. He must learn complete obedience to his teacher, since without obedience the Tao cannot be mastered.

In the case of flower arrangement, it is not entirely accurate to speak of "arrangement." Actually, flowers hate to be arranged. The greatest master of flowers is the one who can think with the flower. He prepares the situation which allows the flower to arrange itself. When someone twists the flowers this way and that, he may achieve a flower arrangement, but this certainly is not the Tao.

Judo, aikido, sado (the Way of Tea) are all Ways—Tao. Students of these skills learn the Way of practice and this is different from ordinary education. In the ordinary classroom the teacher stands in front of the blackboard, talks, and writes while the pupils take notes, pass examinations, and earn credits. As you know, in order to do zazen, we use our spines, our backbones to support us. Along the same lines, Tao practice becomes the backbone of our lives. Ordinary education does not.

In any case, Joshu asked, "What is Tao?" In other words, he was asking, "What is the best Tao to follow as a human being?" This is a wonderful question when viewed both existentially and fundamentally.

Nansen said, "Everyday life is Tao." Our everyday, ordinary life is no other than the Tao.

To this Joshu further queried, "Well, if so, how can I master the

Tao?"

Nansen answered, "The more you try to master it, the more it will evade you." Now, this is a familiar experience for those who do zazen. The more you want to enter into samadhi, the more it will evade you. The more desperately you want to have kensho, the further away it goes.

Finally Joshu asked, "If I do not try to master it or if I do not direct myself to it, how can I know that it is the Tao?" In other words, "How can I know that from washing my face in the morning until falling asleep at night I am living with Tao? How can I know that I am on the right Path?"

Nansen answered, "The Path does not belong to the world of senses. Neither does it belong to a world absent of senses. Knowledge is a delusion and ignorance is senseless."

If I started to explain the Buddhist interpretation of such terms as the world of senses, knowledge, ignorance, etc., it would take hours and hours and we would still not get any place. These terms are not so important to the understanding of this koan. Fundamental reality is another name for Path and it does not belong to any category. But if we, as human beings, want to know what the Path is, we have to do at least two things. Nansen said, "If you want to attain the True Path"—that is, not sticking to phrases, names, sentences and paragraphs—"make yourself as vast and free as the sky. Name it neither good nor not good, as you like."

This is Nansen's suggestion. But I should like to add something more. Let us realize that we human beings are beings of emotion. Emotions include crying, self-pity, envy, fear, the various kinds of love, hate and happiness. Besides emotions, we are beings of karma— karma which we are continually creating with our thoughts, acts and words. Let us realize also that human beings are beings of delusions, fantasies, intellect and intuition—very complicated beings. Animals, on the other hand, are less complicated it seems. Their lives are controlled by their instincts. I have heard that rats, for example, deserted a house three days before it burned down. Also I have heard that a severe winter is predictable when the wild geese from Canada appear in the early fall on Beecher Lake at Dai Bosatsu Zendo. But we human beings, because of our emotions and our judgmental and rationalizing facilities, wear so many layers of underclothes and overclothes to protect ourselves. Thus our minds are not as sharp and clear as they ought to be. Eating meat and fish, drinking alcohol, smoking cigarettes, and so on just serve to add still more layers of clothing. Sesshin, however, gives us the opportunity to shed some of our superfluous garments. "If you want to reach the True Path, make yourself as vast and free as the sky." Don't wear so many layers of clothing.

> How boundless the cleared sky of samadhi!
> How transparent the perfect moonlight of the Fourfold Wisdom!

How transparent we are on the sixth day of sesshin! I am almost sure that all of you have entered this "boundless . . . sky of samadhi." Your hara and this world are no longer separable. You breathe in from hara and breathe out into hara, into the center of the world. There are no boundaries separating yourself from your cushion. There are no borders between yourself and others. If we enter such a free state of mind yet, at the same time, if we realize the clear-cut distinction that self is self and other is other, then we are walking on the Path.

Thus, fundamentally speaking, there is no path apart from our daily lives. But, existentially speaking, a path to follow is needed. And the Path to realize is no other than ceaseless practice on a path. This ceaseless practice gives us confidence in life. It leads us to the realization that all aspects of our lives are the Path itself and cannot be otherwise.

About the dialogue between Nansen and Joshu, Mumon commented:

> Nansen should have resolved Joshu's doubts as soon as Joshu asked the questions. I don't believe that Joshu understood what Nansen meant. He needed at least thirty more years of practice.

Mumon Ekai Zenji (1183–1260), the compiler of The Gateless Gate, often gives comments in what seems a strange way. What seem to be criticisms are actually words of admiration. We may say to a friend, "You are terrible," when actually we mean, "You are wonderful."

In the same way, Mumon's comment is his way of showing his admiration for both masters, especially Joshu's lucid understanding. There is no end to our practice, so in order to encourage us, Mumon said that even the great Joshu "needed at least thirty more years of practice."

Years ago I visited the late Shibayama Zenkei Roshi at his temple, Nanzen-ji in Kyoto. He gave me a *rakusu* and on the back wrote: *Sara ni sanzeyo sanjyu nen*, which means "at least thirty more years of practice." So I asked him, "If I come to you thirty years from now, what will you say?"

"I will give you another rakusu and write: 'At least thirty more years of practice!' "

Mumon's verse describes the four seasons:

> *In spring, hundreds of flowers;*
> *In autumn, a clear full moon;*
> *In summer, a cool breeze;*
> *In winter, snowflakes:*
> *With no hang-ups in your mind,*
> *Every season is a good season!*

When we are free from hang-ups every season is a good season! Every day is a good day. Every event is a good event. This is what Mumon's verse so beautifully describes. Zazen practice is no other than to be free from hang-ups and "make ourselves as vast and free as the sky."

New York Zendo Shobo-ji
January 20, 1977

Seppo's Grain of Rice

The Blue Rock Collection: Case 5

The Koan:
> Master Seppo told his disciples, "When you pick up the whole universe, it is like a grain of rice. I throw it out in front of you fellows and tell you to look. Beat the drum! Call everybody! Search for it!"

The Teisho:
One drama has finished, another is now starting. Life, it seems, is a continuation of drama after drama. Some dramas are very dramatic and some are not. The only difference between the drama in the theater and the drama in life is that drama in life is not allowed a rehearsal. We cannot rehearse and we can never know what will happen. So one of the greatest parts of zazen practice is to be ready, so that no matter what happens, we are in control. And this is why life is never boring. Indeed, it becomes very interesting. Zazen is, indeed, a way of life.

Today's koan is a drama. At the time Seppo was giving this talk, he was not thinking that his teisho would eventually become one of the koans in *The Blue Rock Collection* and that for one thousand years it would be told by numerous teachers to their students. Certainly Seppo had no idea that one day his talk would be translated into English and be told to Dharma friends in the West. So we never know what will be recorded and we never know what will be ignored. This is another interesting part of life.

Seppo Gison Zenji (822–908) said, "When you pick up the whole universe, it is like a grain of rice. I throw it out in front of you fellows and tell you to look. Beat the drum! Call everybody! Search for it!"

Seppo's Dharma successor was Ummon. Ummon said, "Look, this world is vast and wide. Why do you put on your priest's robe at the sound of the bell?"

Ummon said, "This world is vast and wide," but his teacher, Seppo, said, "When you pick up the whole universe, it is like a grain of rice." Why is this? Last night the moon was beautiful and perhaps it will remain so today, tomorrow and the day after tomorrow. When we look up at the sky we can see the moon, many stars, the sun, the clouds, etc. So, in the ordinary sense, Ummon's statement that the world is vast and wide seems to be true. Furthermore, because of modern science we know that there is a solar system made up of the sun and many planets and that there is not only one solar system, but many, many, as it is written in the *Diamond Sutra*. Now, it is rather difficult for us to accept what Seppo said. For beginners, most of the koans give the impression that they are just crazy statements. This is unfortunately the reason why Zen Buddhism is misunderstood. However, this is the interesting part of Zen literature. Suppose a koan philosophically states that every existence is complete, as it is, under any circumstance. Even though this would be true, that koan would have no fragrance, no taste. So when you look at the koans, not only during this teisho, but especially when you are studying them by yourselves for dokusan, it is important for you to be able to see which are the key words of the koan. Each has one, two or three key words. The rest is just fragrance and taste or a camouflage of leaves and branches. Take a simple example:

> A monk asked Joshu, "Has a dog Buddha nature or not?"
> Joshu said, "Mu!"

This koan has only two key words. "Mu" is one and "Buddha nature" is the other.

How about this one?

> Hakuin said, "When you clap two hands, there is a sound. But what is the sound of one hand?"

"One" is the key word here, not "sound." So when you are given a koan, you have to memorize it, repeat it over and over again, and search for what is essential and what is superfluous. If you are well trained you can almost immediately see what is unnecessary and what are the decorations, so to speak.

In today's koan Seppo told his disciples, "When you pick up the whole universe, it is like a grain of rice. I throw it out in front of you fellows and tell you to look. Beat the drum! Call everybody! Search for it!" So what are the key words here? "Throw it out" is not as important as "pick up." "Look" is asking for attention. "The whole universe" is the central theme of our practice regardless of the koan. But the koan also says, ". . . like a grain of rice." Why is this so? This "why" is the way to start to work on your koan.

By the way, this may be slightly beside the point, but some of you believe that thoughts during zazen are evil. It is very important for you to reorganize your brain, to change your attitude toward thoughts. As we inhale and exhale through the nose, we can still hear, see, smell and feel. If all five senses are working perfectly during zazen, why then must only the brain and thoughts be excluded. Mind, body and the five senses have to act. Of course sometimes, when we are concentrating on one point, we neglect to respond to incoming stimuli. Perhaps some of you right now cannot hear the sound of the bulldozer which is working to clear the area just around this new building. But now that I have reminded you, you can hear it. Perhaps some of you smell the incense, but most of you cannot. When you first entered this room, you could smell it clearly. We take things for granted. This is a human habit. Whatever is appealing at first, later on, we tend to forget it. Therefore, if the incense is especially good, it is better to burn just one inch at a time. Otherwise, the rest will be lost without being appreciated. During zazen we are smelling, hearing, seeing and, especially, feeling. So thoughts, too, are natural phenomena. What is not encouraged is to pursue your thoughts. Especially be wary of fantasies and daydreams, for they are attractive. To pursue them is no good. But as for the coming and going of thoughts, there is no choice. Therefore we should not be annoyed with thoughts, and we must not feel guilty about having them and not being able to empty our minds. This does not mean that your zazen is terrible. The idea of hating thoughts must be banished.

If you want to do koan study and work on Seppo's "grain of rice," you should sit down, assume the proper posture, regulate your breath by counting the exhalations from one to ten and then, silently but firmly, repeat over and over again, "the whole universe is as small as a grain of rice," "the whole universe is as small as a grain of rice." Pursuing this, sooner or later you may feel that you yourself are both as large as the universe and as small as a grain of rice. Without this feeling, which is called koan samadhi, koan study is, after all, just another kind of intellectual game and may not have any particular use. You must become this whole universe. In fact, if you repeat the koan again and again, think about it, push it around in your mind and pursue it, since there will be no other thoughts coming around, you will have no choice but to end up with the universe and a grain of rice. Self disappears, time disappears, sangha disappears, all annoying sounds disappear, and only the universe, a small grain of rice, remains. This is the first step of koan study.

The second step is to present to your teacher what you have empirically understood or intuitively felt. The third step is learning how to express your understanding, either verbally or by the use of your total being. You must express it without using dead, explanatory words. But the degree of the depth of zazen differs from student to student. That is why we cannot do real dokusan collectively. It must be done privately, individually. But teisho is different. Up to a certain degree, some sort of explanatory statements must be given. At the same time, some of the essence is left out. This is not done to hide something. There is nothing to hide.

Whatever information may come through one ear may also depart through the other ear. It doesn't remain long. But whatever wisdom you have attained by yourself, you will never forget it. It is yours and very useful throughout your life. So speaking about answers to koans among friends must be prohibited. They should not be discussed and should not be taught. Koans must be practiced, experienced, expressed and infused.

Returning to Seppo's "the whole universe is as small as a grain of rice," a grain of rice is small and so is this cup that I have here. This cup may be small but it is also as big as the universe. What I am telling you now is called an explanation. This cup, once upon a time, was made in China by someone who used clay, water, fire and air. The potter must have learned his technique from friends and from his teacher, otherwise he could have never made such a cup. His teacher must have learned from his teacher and so forth throughout this transmission period. And each teacher must have made mistakes along with discovering something new, such as perfecting this particular shade of blue. And each teacher had to live and to do so, he had to eat rice. And that rice was grown by a farmer and that farmer must have eaten some fish. And that fish was caught either in a net or with a fishing pole. And that fishing pole was made of bamboo and the fishing net was made of cotton or flax. And that flax was made by someone, and so on. So we think that this is just a cup but this tiny cup does, after all, contain the whole universe: heat from the sun, water for the clay and wood for firing the kiln were indispensable. And so this cup, this tiny cup, does certainly contain the whole universe.

This is just a comprehensible explanation, and it is not particularly Zen Buddhism. Anyone can make up any kind of explanation, but at least the point that I was trying to make is that the whole universe is condensed into THIS. We cannot just analyze it. To say that the world is vast and wide is true and to say that the whole universe is extremely tiny is also true. These statements do not contradict each other. There is a Chinese phrase which goes:

On this great earth, I can't find even one speck of soil.

Even one speck of soil doesn't exist. Only this wide world exists. So to say that something is small or that something is big is, after all, saying the same thing in two different ways. East and West is, after all, the same thing. From California, New York is east. But from Japan, New York is west. No one really knows where east starts and where west ends; where north starts and where south ends; where heaven starts and where earth ends. This is the very place where heaven starts. This is the very place, the beginning of heaven, the beginning of earth, the center of the Self. These three elements come together here, in the hara. Heaven is not somewhere over there. If we go to a horizon, there is always another horizon. We can never reach heaven if we search for it outside. We can never reach Truth if we search for it outside. Master Hakuin says:

> *Not knowing how near the Truth is,*
> *We seek it far away—what a pity!*

If we put our minds into hara and sit, we can, without doubt, swallow heaven, we can gulp down the earth. Is this big or small?

The rest of the koan is also interesting. "I throw it in front of you." In a way it cannot be thrown away. Wherever you pick it up, that very place is the whole universe. "Throw away" is what I have been calling the "taste and fragrance," the "leaves and branches" of this koan. Since Seppo said, "pick it up," he therefore said, "throw it away." Get rid of it! Let it go! Throw away your understanding! Throw away your conceptions about heaven and earth! Throw away your ideas about the universe! Heaven is not how I described it. The concept remains, but the essence is gone. Search and search! Of course wherever you search, you will find that there is no such thing as heaven and earth and the universe. But, at the same time, whatever you pick up is the whole universe itself. This is the interesting part of reality. When you understand this matter both intellectually and experientially, then you may speak about the whole universe.

So whatever zazen you are practicing, whether you are counting or watching your breath, working with "Namu Dai Bosa" or "Mu" or "shikantaza," remember that they are just different manifestations of the same thing, like the waves in the ocean. The waves may differ, but the ocean keeps its essence. Always keep your mind in your hara! Melt yourself into the universe and realize your true nature!

Dai Bosatsu Zendo Kongo-ji
October 16, 1975

Ummon's Good Day

The Blue Rock Collection: Case 6

The Koan:
On the middle day of the month, Master Ummon said to his disciples,
"I do not ask you anything about before the fifteenth day of the month.
Say something about after the fifteenth day of the month!"
As none of the disciples could answer, Ummon answered himself,
"Every day is a good day!"

The Teisho:
Having sat for six days, our spiritual strength is fully restored. Already this is the last day of sesshin. Our powers extend over the ten quarters and through the three periods of time, and we are strong. Indeed, strong! The more we sit, the stronger we become. As to revolving the wheel of Dharma, let no thought be wasted over it. May all beings attain true wisdom.

> *However innumerable all beings are,*
> *We vow to save them all;*
> *However inexhaustible delusions are,*
> *We vow to extinguish them all;*
> *However immeasurable the Dharma Teachings are,*
> *We vow to master them all;*
> *However endless the Buddha's Way is,*
> *We vow to follow it.*

What more need I say!
As I was brought up with the understanding that praise spoils people, I don't usually speak about how wonderful you are and how nicely you are doing. As long as you don't hear from me, you may assume that I

am admiring you and that everything is okay. Even if I say something critical, don't interpret it in the ordinary way. Take it as encouragement to grow more. In the samurai tradition, praise is considered to be poison.

We sit at least fifty minutes, sometimes fifty-five minutes or even one hour. Though you may be struggling with excruciating pain, nobody moves to disturb the quiet. The zendo takes on a sharp atmosphere. As a result of this kind of strong sitting for nearly seven consecutive days, I am happy to tell you that many of my beloved friends have tasted and testified to something which we have been talking about for years.

Zen Buddhism was born in China. Originally, Zen Buddhism came from India, but it was in China that both samadhi (deep stillness) and prajna (wisdom) were equally stressed. Therefore, the language used by the old masters to express their Zen was Chinese. But English is good enough as long as the English-speaking Dharma student is able to develop his understanding of Zen Buddhism enough to express it as well as Ummon, Joshu or Rinzai did in Chinese. The time has come when we have to cook our own food instead of taking it out from a Chinese restaurant.

We are all Dharma pioneers. The frontier age of Zen Buddhism in America is happening right now. Frankly speaking, we cannot expect any more Japanese monks. They may come and they may not. So actually you are the ones who, not only being content with your own samadhi and realization, must leave something for the coming generations, either by the written word or by transmitting it from heart to heart. But some parts of the practice cannot be described, like how to strike the *inkin* (the bell which marks the beginning and end of a sitting), the duration between strikes and the strength of each strike. This is one of the transmissions, so to speak. The sound of the gong, the bell, the clappers, and the speed of the mokugyo, etc., are important since with the right combination of these instruments, the zendo atmosphere becomes sharp. That sharpness of atmosphere makes our zazen more lucid. Those of you who really have the Bodhisattva Vow had better start seriously thinking of yourselves as the fathers and mothers of American Zen Buddhism.

Suppose in a monastery in present-day Japan there are one hundred monks. I should estimate that eighty-five of them are there because they are themselves the sons of temple priests. After staying about two or three years, they return to their fathers' temples and assume the rather mundane routines of a temple priest.

Now look at America! Suppose we have one hundred Zen students here at Dai Bosatsu Zendo. None of them have fathers who are temple priests and none are therefore obliged to stay for a certain number of years in order to succeed them. So the Japanese Zen students' motivation indeed differs greatly from their American counterparts. Since this is the frontier generation, some of us stay here at Dai Bosatsu Zendo for years, later going to some distant place to start his or her own zazen group. This is one possibility. Another possibility is if you have to move away because of family or work, you may return here from time to time, making this place your spiritual home. Or you may stay here for good, for the sake of good. Or, just like what most of you are doing in New York City, you have your own work, but you come to the New York Zendo regularly to continue your practice part-time.

In any case, it is extremely important for us to be aware of where we stand. I think that American Zen will grow in the American way, using the English language. There will eventually be no need to translate from Sanskrit, Chinese or Japanese. The main point is that Zen Buddhism does not depend on words and phrases. Rather, it directly points to the True Nature of ourselves.

Prepare yourselves to be independent. All you need is sangha harmony. It is hard, so hard for us not to think of ourselves first. But at least let us try.

Now about Ummon Bun'en Zenji (862/4–949): he lived during the last part of the T'ang Dynasty and is especially known for his unique, elegant, refined and poetic way of expressing his Zen. Here are some of his responses:

> Ummon told his monks: "Each of you is the light itself, but when you become self-conscious, the light becomes dark. Now tell me, what is the light?"

No monk answered. Ummon therefore said, "However wonderful a thing is, it may be that it is better not to have it at all."

Ummon said to his monks: "Medicine and sickness are mutually dependent. Look! The entire universe is nothing but medicine. Now tell me, what is your Self?"

A monk asked Ummon, "What is the teaching of Buddha?"
Ummon said, "Tai issetsu!—Be with it!"

And today's masterpiece:

"Every day is a good day!"

In Ummon's time the lunar calendar was in use. Therefore, every month had exactly thirty days. At that time, too, Zen teachers did not use any teisho texts because there were no such things as teisho texts. Every day was a text-making Dharma battle.

"I do not ask anything about before the fifteenth day of the month!" If Ummon had simply said, "I don't ask about the past, but tell me about the present and the future," he would have been guilty of lack of fragrance and taste and perhaps this whole incident may have been quickly forgotten.

Every day the moon becomes larger and larger and on the fifteenth day, it becomes full. This is one aspect of reality, and let us call it "the reality of progress." Compared with the way we were in the past, we have been making progress, of one sort or another. This tangible present is better than the past, since the ungraspable past exists only in memory.

As we are concerned with Mind, let me point out the fact that the moon is always full, whether we can see it or not. Let's call this "the reality of as-it-is-ness." Nothing is lacking, nothing is superfluous. Even the crescent moon is a full moon, since, as it is, it is perfect as the crescent moon. Since only a part of the moon can be seen from earth, we are deluded into thinking that it increases and decreases in size. But the plain fact is, whether we can see it or not, whether we call it new moon, half-moon or crescent moon, the moon is full—ALWAYS!

This reality of as-it-is-ness is no other than Mind. Zazen practice leads us to the reality of as-it-is-ness.

To speak of "the reality of progress" and "the reality of as-it-is-ness" is not postulating any kind of dualism. Although people may think that these two realities exist apart from each other, this is not so. It is this kind of thinking which leads to confusion.

The mind of "the reality of progress" has many aspects: spiritual, mental, psychological, emotional, etc. They are all interrelated. When external things move favorably, we feel good. But when they do not go in the way that we want, we feel miserable. This happens again and again. Not only do external things not always happen according to our preference, but people, too, often do not behave as we would like them to. When this happens we complain and even try to change them so that they will suit our egotistic preferences. But can we change another person's ideology? Can we change another person's personality? Can we change the climate? Can we stop the rain and ask the sun to stay as long as we wish? These things are almost impossible to change. But there is one thing that we can do, and that is, we can change our attitude. Instead of hating unfavorable surroundings, accept them as they are. When this is done, anger becomes less and joy grows. Who then will become happy? The more we are able to accept people and things as they are, the more we grow spiritually. The more we grow spiritually, the more "good days" we will have.

As always, today's koan should be interpreted from the point of view of the reality of as-it-is-ness. It was the full-moon night (maybe it was not, but let us assume so because that would give this story a more poetic atmosphere). "I don't ask about the past fifteen days. Tell me about the coming fifteen days." Or Ummon could have said, "I don't ask about your immature time, but having done zazen and having clear insight like:

> How boundless the cleared sky of samadhi!
> How transparent the perfect moonlight of the
>   Fourfold Wisdom!
> At this moment what more need we seek?
> As the Truth eternally reveals itself,

> *This very place is the Lotus Land of Purity,*
> *This very body is the body of the Buddha.*

now say something!"

Luckily, no monk could open his mouth, so the eternal master-piece, "every day is a good day," came out from Ummon's mouth. Every day is a good day! What a masterpiece! It's as perfect as Joshu's Mu. You may think perhaps that yesterday was a terrible day, that today is just so-so, that the day before yesterday was just fair and that, hopefully, tomorrow night will be very good. But "every day is a good day!" Repeat this phrase time and again for encouragement.

Look at the present! There is no time but now! There is no place but here! Understanding this plain factuality, we can perhaps say what Ummon said, but in a different way. Adjectives confuse us, adverbs become impediments and prepositions lead us astray—put them aside! And now pretend that you are one of Ummon's disciples. How would you answer his question: "I don't ask you anything about before the the fifteenth day of the month. Say something about after the fifteenth day of the month!"

"Today is October 18th!"

How about this answer? Is today a good day? Is today a bad day? Is today October 17 or 19? *Today is October 18th!* Nothing more, nothing less. This is what I call "GOOD."

> *"What is the samadhi of each individual thing?"*
> *Ummon said, "Rice in bowl, water in pail!"*

Ummon's answer sounds okay, but it's not good enough. What would you say? How about: RICE! BOWL! WATER! PAIL! When you are able to pick out what is superfluous, then you can make your understanding sharp and clear. When you clean your room, all you have to do is remove the dust.

So tonight we will sit, sit, sit! The more we sit, the stronger we become. The energy of the universe somehow comes into us. During the first day of the sesshin, this was not possible. Now it is! Time is so precious. Waste it not!

Do your best!

Dai Bosatsu Zendo Kongo-ji
October 18, 1975

Rinzai's Gold Dust

The Recorded Sayings of Master Rinzai: Dialogues

The Koan:

One day Councilor O visited Master Rinzai. When he met the Master in front of the zendo he asked, "Do the monks of your monastery read the sutras?"

"No, they don't read sutras," replied the Master.

"Then do they practice zazen?"

"No, they don't practice zazen."

"If they neither read sutras nor practice zazen, what in the world are they doing?"

"All I do is make them become Buddhas and patriarchs."

The councillor said, "Though gold dust is precious, when it gets into the eyes, it clouds the vision."

"I used to think that you are just an ordinary man, but now I know that you are not," said the Master.

The Teisho:

Yesterday someone left a piece of paper on my cushion in the zendo. On it was written a kind of haiku:

Rohatsu Fifth Night

> *All tracks*
> *Now covered with snow*
> *Along this mountain road.*

Tracks, traces—black part of the road, brown part of the road, high part of the road, low part of the road . . . . All are now covered with white snow—one color and one level. I think that this is what the author of this beautiful haiku was trying to say. But the word "covered" bothered me. What we are doing in zazen practice is not covering up. A word like "melted," instead of "covered," catches more appropriately the spirit of sesshin. We are not covering anything. Rather, we are trying to melt our concept of ego.

This reminds me of one of Rinzai Gigen Zenji's (d. 866) sermons. Master Rinzai said:

Followers of the Way, if you want insight into Dharma, as it is, just don't be deluded by others. Whatever you encounter, slay it at once. Upon meeting a Buddha, slay the Buddha; upon meeting a patriarch, slay the patriarch; upon meeting an arhat, slay the arhat; upon meeting your parents, slay your parents. And you will attain emancipation.

When you hear this kind of advice you may become confused unless you know how to read Zen texts, that is, you must learn how to find the key point. Then what is the key point of Master Rinzai's sermon? It is neither "Buddha," "patriarch," "arhat" nor "parents." The key point is "slay." In fact, what we do during zazen—for example, repeating Mu-u-u-u, Mu-u-u-u—is no other than Rinzai's "slay," or more precisely, cutting through.

Although Rinzai said that if you meet the Buddha or patriarchs, slay them, while we are walking on a busy street none of us will meet Buddhas or patriarchs. But for sure, even on a country road where no one else is walking, we are always encountering the self. This self is our best friend and our worst enemy. This self is our best supporter and our worst destroyer. Once my teacher, Soen Roshi, said:

I love myself the most; I hate myself the most.

And Nyogen Senzaki said:

We can separate from a good friend, but we cannot separate from the self. We can leave our parents, but we cannot leave the self. We can divorce our husbands and wives, but we cannot divorce the self.

"Followers of the Way, if you meet the Buddha, slay him." Slay the ego! Slay pride! Slay all thoughts! This is the essential point of zazen practice.

During morning service we chant:

BUDDHAM SARANAM GACCHAMI
DHAMMAN SARANAM GACCHAMI
SANGHAM SARANAM GACCHAMI

I take refuge in the Buddha
I take refuge in the Dharma
I take refuge in the Sangha

Now this is of course important. Taking refuge requires religious faith and devotion. But by the sixth day of sesshin you can understand "religious" in the purest sense of the word. Faith and devotion are not as essential as "slay." Slay the Buddha! Slay the Dharma! Slay the Sangha! Cut through! Cut through! We must cut through our concepts of Buddha, as such, of Dharma, as such, of Sangha, as such.

In general, religion is quite misunderstood. But after having sat for six days in this Rohatsu Sesshin, we can understand the true meaning and spirit of religion. Etymologically, the word religion consists of two elements: the prefix *re*, which means "back" or "again," and the Latin root *ligare*, which means "to bind" or "to unite." Even prior to heaven and earth, there was no God, as such. It was not God who created the world. It is our minds that conceive of a beginning and an end. Therefore, it was our minds that created the Creation and created a God apart from ourselves. In this way, we separated ourselves from God. So fundamentally, religion is not a matter of worshiping God. Rather, it is a matter of returning to the "united" or once again realizing the undivided condition. This is religious experience.

How does zazen practice relate to the essential quality of religion as I have just described it? To state it briefly, zazen is no other than the process of slaying—slaying the subject and the object; slaying the division between God and Creation. Although the word "slay" may seem to some people a strange and even dangerous expression, if we take a gentle and safe attitude, nothing can be accomplished. Therefore I sternly say to you, "Work hard!" instead of saying, "Would you be good enough to do Mu for a while?"

"Slay the Buddha!" "Slay the patriarchs!" "Slay the arhats!" Indeed, speaking in this manner is going to extremes and I would not even think of doing so during a regular lecture in a classroom. If this tape is ever transcribed and if someone who has never had sesshin experience casually reads it, he may conclude that I am a very dangerous man. But being here now, it is easy for you to understand what I mean. This is one of the greatest virtues of participating in sesshin and doing Mu . . . .

Getting back to the haiku . . . Melt! Slay! But do not cover up!

As long as I am speaking about something apart from today's koan, I might as well say a little more. By now, the sixth day of Rohatsu Sesshin, I am sure that all of you understand that losing and finding do not at all contradict each other. In our everyday lives we think that losing and finding are two different matters. Through our zazen experience we realize that as much as we lose, we find. We know that losing *is* finding.

In order to clarify this point, let me give you an example. Suppose I am a sculptor and I intend to carve a Buddha statue from a piece of wood. The more wood I carve away (the more I lose), the more clearly the Buddha image appears (the more I find). It is not that I have to add something from the outside. Rather, only by losing do I find. This is a wonderful realization. Even though you may think that "realization" is somewhere outside, this *is* realization. We often speak about freedom. If this is not freedom—that is, freedom from the idea that losing and finding are not contradictory—then what is real freedom? If we have been bounded by the thought of the separation of losing and finding, now we are emancipated. We are all free and enlightened.

The means to the end and the end itself are the same thing. The process is the goal and the goal is the process. We just think that everything has a beginning, a middle and an end. And when we reach the so-called "end," we think that we will achieve a "goal." Nevertheless, none of us thinks that the goal of life is death. The goal of life is to truly live. The process is the goal.

This is also true of zazen practice. Each Mu and each breath, *this very moment and this very place*, have been the goal, are the goal and will always be the goal. The Way is endless, but *each* moment we are at home, *each* moment is the goal. The means and the end, the process and the goal are not separate from each other. If emancipation from ordinary, dualistic thinking is not emancipation, then what is? You may expect that when you are emancipated extraordinary events will take place. Heaven and earth will turn upside down. Slay these expectations! Getting rid of such thinking is emancipation itself.

So one day Councilor O visited Master Rinzai. Most likely, both of them were taking a walk. When they came to the front of the zendo, Councilor O asked Master Rinzai, "Do the students in this monastery study the *Heart Sutra*?"

"No."

"Do they practice zazen?"

"No."

"If they don't study sutras and if they don't practice zazen, what in the world do they do?"

"All I do is make them become Buddhas and patriarchs."

Then Councilor O said, "No matter how precious gold may be, when the dust of it gets into the eyes, it clouds the vision."

This is a wonderful expression. With admiration Master Rinzai immediately said, "I thought you were just an ordinary fellow, but now I see that you are not."

This dialogue may need some explanation. Of course, as long as there is a Zen Buddhist monastery, there is sutra chanting and the students must learn to master it. Of course, the zendo is a place to do nothing but zazen. It is so obvious. Why then did Master Rinzai say "No," and what is the meaning of "All I do is make them become Buddhas and patriarchs"?

Every day we recite:

All beings are primarily Buddha. . .

and

As for zazen practice in the Mahayana, we have no words to praise it fully . . .

This is true, but no matter how many times we may recite: "All beings are primarily Buddha" and "As for zazen practice in the Mahayana, we have no words to praise it fully," they are no more than sayings. To say and to do are two different things. A description of something has no life, no impact. We may say that ice is cold, but only when we have actually touched ice does the word "cold" take on life. This is the difference between the description and the action, saying and doing. So instead of giving Councilor O a long, descriptive, dead lecture, Rinzai said, "No, they don't." Then he said, "All I do is make them become Buddha." Are not all beings primarily Buddha? How can the Buddha become more Buddha?

Councilor O said, "Though gold dust is precious. . . ." It is precious to become a Buddha. It is precious to do zazen and sutra study does have great merit. But when these things are just talked about or just described, they lose their preciousness, they lose their merit. In the same way, though it is precious to say that we are primarily Buddha or that we will all become Buddhas and patriarchs, when these statements are spoken to a person who has opened his Dharma eye, they become dead phrases, they "cloud the vision."

Rinzai said, "I thought you were an ordinary fellow, but now I understand that you are not."

Now this is a wonderful dialogue—nothing special. But it is important for all of us to remember:

> Though gold dust is precious, when it gets into the eyes, it clouds the vision.

Zazen is nothing more special than learning this simple matter. How? There are no shortcuts, no secrets. Just sit more! Sit more!

There are not so many monasteries that practice Rohatsu Sesshin as precisely as we do. Only forty-eight hours to go. Do your best!

Dai Bosatsu Zendo Kongo-ji
December 6, 1977

APPENDIX

Rohatsu Exhortation

by
Hakuin Ekaku Zenji

Translated by Eido Tai Shimano

The First Night:

Master Hakuin said, "It is essential for you, a student of Dharma who practices zazen, first of all to sit down on a thick cushion in full-lotus posture, loosen your robe and belt, straighten your spine, and then calm your body and mind. Then begin to count your breath, from one to ten, in taut silence. To enter deep samadhi, this is incomparably the best way.

"As you fill up your hara with zazen energy, start working on your koan with an intensive mind, cutting through all thoughts. If you continue to practice zazen day after day without cease, even if you should miss striking the ground, you cannot fail to experience kensho. Don't you want that?

"Do your best!"

The Second Night:

Master Hakuin said, "A sutra says:

When one attains True Realization, he is not only united with the ten directions of the world, but he is also united with the whole sangha in the Enlightened Mind.

"Wherever the practice of zazen takes place, there is a Deity of Protection and a Deity of Disturbance. For instance, when many people come together, even to worship God, among them there are usually a few pickpockets. When a student's motivation and 'Great

Vows for All,' are strong and his commitment is firm, the Deity of Protection becomes strong and supports his sitting. When, on the other hand, a student's mind is wandering, the Deity of Disturbance becomes strong. For this reason, it is crucial for you students of Dharma to cultivate the Bodhisattva Spirit. Upholding the 'Great Vows for All,' with a humble spirit, dedicate this zazen to all other beings. The Deity of Protection supports your practice.

"The Ultimate Reality of Buddha-Dharma can never be actualized without the most forceful vow. That vow needs patience, perseverance and endurance. It is like the practice of archery. In the beginning you won't be able to hit the bull's-eye, but if you patiently continue to practice, your body will master the action. The practice of zazen is analogous. Breath after breath, *nen* after *nen*, concentrate your total being to penetrate Mu. If you do and if you do not give up, all the Dharma cannot but be revealed in front of you. To attain Buddhahood is as easy as picking up the dust off the floor.

"Do your best!"

The Third Night:

Master Hakuin said, "There are two kinds of Bodhisattvas: some transmit the Buddha-Dharma, others protect the Buddha-Dharma. The relationship between these two Bodhisattvas is just like that between a master and his students. When they are not in harmony, the Dharma light will not shine brightly. Transmission of the Dharma and protection of the Dharma are equally important.

"Zazen is the essence of all culture and the essence of all the ways to practice. The Shinto tradition says that our body and mind are the condensation of Heaven and Earth, and Heaven and Earth are the expansion of our body and mind. Seven heavenly deities, five earthly deities, eight hundred thousand other deities reside nowhere but in our very body and mind. In order to serve them in the proper way, zazen is the indispensable practice. Buddhism, Shintoism and many other teachings speak about samadhi. Zen Buddhism, however, especially emphasizes the absolute necessity of its practice. Erect your spine! Fill your hara with zazen energy! Whatever you hear, whatever you see, pursue not the thought. When your six sense organs are purified, you are serving the deities. Even for one sitting, the virtue of it is immeasurable. Master Dogen said:

A day of diligence is a day of preciousness, and a hundred years of laziness are a hundred years of regret.

"Be careful and be mindful!"

The Fourth Night:
Master Hakuin said, "There are six wonderful ways to breathe. They are *su* (to count), *zui* (to follow), *shi* (to stop), *kan* (to see), *gen* (to forget), *jo* (to purify). *Su* means just to count your breath and enter into counting samadhi. After having counted the breath for a while, just follow each breath, letting them come by themselves. This is *zui*. Although there are six different ways to breathe, these two, counting and following, are essential.

"Bodhidharma said:

Outwardly do not connect your breath with the thought of what is happening. Inwardly do not interfere with the flow of the breath. Just free yourself from all incoming thoughts, and hold your mind against them like a great iron wall. Then enter samadhi.

"To 'just free yourself from all incoming thoughts' means that you should not cling, to them. To 'hold your mind against them like a great iron wall,' means to go straight ahead.

"Followers of the Way, this verse has profound meaning. Try to sit as intensively as you can, as if to break through a great iron wall. Bravely march on! Believe me, even if you should miss striking the ground, you cannot miss attaining kensho.

"Do your best! Do your *very* best!"

The Fifth Night:
Master Hakuin said, "Usually there are three lengths of training periods in the monastery. The longest is one hundred twenty days, the next is one hundred days, and the shortest is ninety days. During these

periods, participants strive to clarify THIS matter. No one is allowed to leave the monastery, and no one speaks unnecessarily.

"In the practice of zazen a daring, courageous attitude is essential. Let me tell you a story. Recently there lived a man named Heishiro. He carved a stone Buddha and placed it near a waterfall in the deep mountains. Then he happened to sit down by the pool at the bottom of the waterfall. He noticed a lot of bubbles in the stream. After falling, some of the bubbles disappeared quickly and some disappeared after running ten feet or more. While he was looking at them, due to his karma, he strongly felt the transiency of life. He realized that all phenomena, good or bad, are just like the bubbles on the surface of the water. The impact of this realization made him feel the worthlessness of just living, just spending days without understanding the mystery of life.

"By chance, he heard someone reading out loud from the sayings of Master Takusui:

The man of sympathy and bravery deserves enlightenment, but for the man of indolence, realization of his True Nature will never come.

"Inspired by this saying, Heishiro went into a small room and locked the door. He sat down, erected his spine, clasped his hands in a fist and opened his eyes widely. With a pure straightforward mind, he did zazen. Innumerable thoughts, delusions and hallucinations appeared. But his zazen defeated them all, and he reached a deep and calm state of thoughtlessness. He continued to sit through the night. At dawn, when he heard the birds singing outside, he could not find his body. He felt as if his eyes had fallen to the ground. A moment later, he felt the pain of his fingernails digging into his hands and then realized that his eyes had come back to their usual place. He was able to stand up and walk. He repeated this kind of zazen for three days and nights. On the morning of the fourth day, after washing his face, he looked at the trees in the garden. They appeared so different. He felt strange. Heishiro did not understand this, so he visited a neighborhood priest. But the priest was himself helpless to explain. At someone's suggestion, Heishiro came to see me [Hakuin]. On the way to my monastery, he had to climb to the top of a mountain. Suddenly, he looked at the panoramic view of the seashore. It was at that moment that he thoroughly understood that all beings, grasses, trees, land and birds are primarily Buddha. Excitedly, he came to my dokusan room and immediately passed several important koans.

"Now let us remember that Heishiro was merely an ordinary man. He did not know anything about Zen nor had he practiced zazen. Nevertheless, through only three days and nights of intensive sitting, he was able to unite his being with all others and to clarify the meaning of his being. It was his motivation and his daring, courageous attitude that had overcome all obstacles.

"Brothers and sisters of the Dharma, why don't you have such strong determination?

"Bravely work hard!"

The Sixth Night:

As an attendant monk had just brought him a cup of tea, Master Hakuin said, "When Myoan Yosai Zenji was in China, once he became sick from the heat. An old Chinese man gave him some green tea, and he soon recovered. Remembering this event with gratitude, he brought some green tea seeds back from China to Japan and planted them in Uji, near Kyoto. Myoan Yosai Zenji was the first person to introduce tea to our nation.

"The essence of tea is bitterness. This bitterness is good for the heart. When the heart is strong, the rest of the inner organs will be healthy.

"An old sage said:

Tea wakes us up and helps our practice. Students of Zen should drink it every day. It also helps to make the mind clear and cheerful when our practice is painful.

"Hard practice, like the bitterness of tea, is not actually bitter or hard. It is the way to straighten our minds and make them more and more lucid. All the ancient Zen masters experienced wonderful self-realization after hard work and sincere practice. So you must do zazen with all your might.

"Recently a priest named Bunmei came to see me. He said that he had been preparing for six years to come here to receive my guidance. When I first met him I said to him, 'Although you are of the highest rank of the priesthood and are allowed to wear a purple robe, if your Dharma eye is not yet opened, I will have to regard you as a new-comer. You will have to get rid of the pride of being a purple-robed priest. Then you will be ready to do zazen.'

"Bunmei answered, 'I consider myself just an ordinary monk, the some as the others. In order that I may understand the true meaning of the Tathagata, will you please guide me with your compassion? I welcome your stick and I am not afraid, even to die!'

"I therefore permitted him to come to dokusan.

"During the one-hundred-day training period, he did zazen daunt-lessly. He received innumerable keisaku from me. As a result, he was able to understand the real meaning of the Tathagata, that is, the real meaning of his life, and he became my Dharma successor. This is a good example of how a brave attitude, sincere practice and total com-mitment make our practice successful.

"Face Mu! Be with it!"

The Seventh Night:

Master Hakuin said, "In Buddhism there is a saying that if a person becomes a monk or a sincere lay student of Dharma, nine generations of his family will be emancipated. To become a true monk or a sincere lay student of Dharma means to have a strong vow to save all beings and to practice bravely. When one disciplines himself in such a way, the vivid Dharma nature appears in front of him and inexpressible joy is with him.

"Long ago there lived a woman near Kyoto. When she conceived, she made a vow that if the baby were a boy, she would have him become a monk. On that very night, an old man appeared to her in a dream and told her, 'I am one of the ancestors of your family, nine generations before you. After my death I went to Hell and suffered unspeakably. However, upon hearing your vow tonight, I was emancipated from the sufferings of Hell.'

"Here is another story: There was once a priest named Ryozen who lived near Mt. Fuji and who ran a Zen group. According to tradition, in December he held a Rohatsu Sesshin and sat with his students. One night while he was sitting, his late mother appeared to him with a knife and pierced his armpit, Ryozen screamed loudly, spat up blood and fainted. But soon he was revived. The next morning, without telling anyone, he left his students and his zendo and started on a pilgrimage. He carried only one meal bowl and three robes. He ate little food and slept under the trees. He visited masters, asking about the Tao. Years passed and his samadhi ripened.

"Once when he was about to enter samadhi, his late mother appeared. When he opened his eyes wide, she disappeared. In time, he was able at last to enter a profound samadhi, as calm as a great ocean. His mother appeared again and told him, 'After my death, I went to Hell. But all the demons respected me and took care of me, saying that I was the mother of a Buddhist monk. It was very comfortable. I never suffered. However, later, when you became old, the demons said that I was not the mother of a monk with true understanding, but the mother of an ordinary man. Angrily, they put me to torture. I hated you furiously, and therefore when you were with your students during your Rohatsu Sesshin, I wanted to kill you. But you left the temple and began your pilgrimage. Once, as you remember, I came to see you. Your samadhi was not yet ripe and you still had many thoughts. So I disappeared. Now you have entered genuine samadhi and found true wisdom. My agonies have ended, and I can go to Heaven. Therefore, I have come today to thank you for your honesty and diligent practice.'

"Each of you has a mother and a father, brothers and sisters and many relatives. If you were to count all of your relatives and ancestors, each one of you would find that you have tens of thousands of them. Many have passed away already and are transmigrating through the six worlds receiving unspeakable suffering. They await your samadhi and realization as keenly as a person in the desert waits for a drop of rain. You cannot sit and daydream. Think of the importance of your mission. Time passes like an arrow and does not wait for us.

"Be diligent! Be diligent!"

The Song of Zazen
(Zazen Wasan)

by
Hakuin Ekaku Zenji

Translated by Eido Tai Shimano

Sentient beings are primarily all Buddhas:
It is like ice and water,
Apart from water no ice can exist.
Outside sentient beings, where do we find the Buddhas?

Not knowing how near the Truth is,
We seek it far away—what a pity!
We are like a man who, in the midst of water,
Cries in thirst so imploringly;
We are like the son of a rich man
Who wandered away among the poor.

The reason why we transmigrate through the six worlds
Is that we are lost in the darkness of ignorance;
Going astray further and further in the darkness,
When are we able to be free from birth and death?

As for zazen practice in the Mahayana,
We have no words to praise it fully:
The virtues of perfection such as charity, morality,
And the invocation of the Buddha's name,
Confession, and ascetic discipline,
And many other good deeds of merit—
All these return into THIS.

Even those who have practiced it for just one sitting
Will see all their evil karma erased;
Nowhere will they find evil paths,
But the Pure Land will be near at hand.

With a reverential heart, if we listen to this Truth
    Even once,
And praise it, and gladly embrace it,
We will surely be blessed most infinitely.
But, if we concentrate within
And testify to the truth that Self-Nature is no-nature,
We have really gone beyond foolish talk.

The gate of the oneness of cause and effect is opened;
The path of non-duality and non-trinity runs
    Straight ahead.

To regard the form of no-form as form,
Whether going or returning, we cannot be any
    Place else;
To regard the thought of no-thought as thought;
Whether singing or dancing, we are the voice of
    The Dharma.

How boundless the cleared sky of samadhi!
How transparent the perfect moonlight of the
    Fourfold Wisdom!

At this moment what more need we seek?
As the Truth eternally reveals itself,
This very place is the Lotus Land of Purity,
This very body is the Body of the Buddha.

Glossary

Editor's Note: With a few exceptions, the following definitions were reproduced from *NAMU DAI BOSA: A Transmission of Zen Buddhism to America* by Nyogen Senzaki, Soen Nakagawa, Eido Shimano (The Bhaisajaguru Series, Theater Arts Books: New York, 1976).

ALAYA (ALAYAVIJNANA): In Buddhist philosophy, alaya (*araya, arayashiki, J.*) is the eighth of the eight consciousnesses and is often referred to as the repository or store consciousness, because in it all experiences are contained and recorded.

ARHAT: An enlightened being in the Hinayana-Theravada tradition of Buddhism. The ideal of the arhat was replaced by that of the Bodhisattva in the Mahayana tradition.

BODHISATTVA: *Bosatsu* or *bosa* in Japanese; literally, *bodhi* means "enlightened" and *sattva* means "being." A Bodhisattva is one who realizes that all beings—not just human beings, even a speck of dust—are primarily Buddhas (enlightened ones), and seeks to share the joy of this realization with others so they themselves may experience this truth. Although it is commonly said that Bodhisattvas postpone their own emancipation until all sentient beings have been saved, the plain fact is that a Bodhisattva cannot help others unless he himself is enlightened; the real driving power behind his work derives from his own realization. Nonetheless, the Bodhisattva is not concerned with his own enlightenment as an end in itself, but as a way of bringing about universal liberation from delusion and suffering. The Bodhisattva ideal is the heart of Mahayana Buddhism.

BUDDHA: Literally "enlightened one." There are many different points of view from which one can speak of "Buddha." Historically the term refers to Siddhartha Gautama, or Shakyamuni Buddha (563–483 B.C.), the actual founder of Buddhism in India. But in an extended sense, Shakyamuni Buddha is not the only Buddha; in Hakuin Zenji's *Zazen Wasan* we read: "Sentient beings are primarily all Buddhas." To this can be added—not just sentient beings; all beings, animate and inanimate, are enlightened ones. There is also the traditional Buddhist doctrine of Trikaya, or "Three Bodies of Buddha." This refers to the Buddha's three principal metaphysical conditions: as the altogether formless Dharmakaya, or Ultimate Reality itself (in the Zen tradition known as Buddha nature or Mu); as the Sambhogakaya, the form in which Buddha appears to preach to Bodhisattvas; and the Nirmanakaya, the infinitely many concrete manifestations of the Buddha in accordance with the needs of sentient beings. (Shakyamuni Buddha can be spoken of as a Nirmanakaya Buddha.) Buddha can also be viewed from the point of view of the Three Treasures, the others being Dharma and Sangha.

DHARANI: An invocation, like a mantra, which is chanted to deepen samadhi. It has been called "the embodiment of a power in sound."

DHARANI OF THE GREAT COMPASSIONATE ONE: *Daihishu* in Japanese; one of the most frequently chanted dharanis in Rinzai Zen Buddhism. For an English translation, see D. T. Suzuki's *Manual of Zen Buddhism.*

DHARMA: *Dhamma* in Pali; the first meaning is "phenomenon." Phenomena appear and disappear, according to the law of causation; hence the second meaning, "law." This is a fact; hence the third meaning, "truth." Finally, since Buddhist teaching is based on this truth, the fourth meaning of Dharma is "teaching."

DHARMAKAYA: The formless form of the Dharma; the condition of the Buddha as identical with ultimate reality itself. There are many Zen koans regarding this matter; the most famous one is Master Joshu's Mu.

DIAMOND SUTRA: Known in Sanskrit as the *Vajracchedika Prajnaparamita Sutra (Kongo Kyo, J.)*, it is one of the two most important sutras of the Prajnaparamita literature (the *Heart Sutra* is the other). The work took its present form in the fourth century; its essential doctrine that all things are "empty" or "void" (sunyata) is a fundamental Buddhist teaching.

DOKUSAN: The private confrontation with a roshi in his room or residence. In the Rinzai tradition, dokusan, or sanzen, is extremely important; according to this school, zazen with frequent dokusan is the most effective Zen practice.

GASSHO: The gesture of putting the palms together to express gratitude. It is used by Buddhists throughout the world as a gesture of greeting as well.

HAIKU: A seventeen-syllable Japanese poem.

HAN: In Zen monasteries, a wooden board struck rhythmically three times a day: dawn, twilight and before retiring. Its dimensions are, approximately, one foot by one and a half feet by three inches. Occasionally this verse is inscribed on it:

> *Listen, O monks!*
> *Be attentive with your practice*
> *Time goes like an arrow.*
> *It doesn't wait for you.*

HARA: Also known as *kikai tanden*, the belly or lower abdominal area, it is the physical center of the body and the most vital region for many forms of meditation. Keeping one's mind in one's hara means to regulate the breath so that it is focused in this area. The resulting accumulation of samadhi energy is essential to zazen practice.

HEART SUTRA: Known in Sanskrit as the *Hridaya Prajnaparamita Sutra* (*Hanna Shin Gyo, J.*), it is, in one sense, a condensed form of the *Diamond Sutra*. Because of its relatively short length, it is a favorite sutra for daily chanting in both Zen and Tibetan Buddhist monasteries. The name Heart is particularly applicable since this sutra sets forth the "heart" or "essence" of the prajnaparamita, or "perfection of wisdom" teachings.

INKIN: A small bell with a handle used in the zendo to indicate the beginning and end of zazen periods.

INO: In Rinzai Zen monasteries, the monk who leads the sutras; in the Soto tradition, the ino is the head monk of the monastery.

JIKIJITSU: The leader of zazen in a Rinzai zendo, he is responsible for maintaining discipline and for encouraging and inspiring students.

KARMA: Literally "action." Karma is usually identified with the law of cause and effect as it operates in the moral and physical domain. But in a broader sense everything is karma itself. Karma is not limited by time and space, nor is it something exclusively individual; there is collective karma. The three sources of karma are said to be body, mouth and thought. Associated with karma is the idea of the continuity of life and death. In the deepest sense, karma is energy, and as the modern physical principle states, matter cannot be destroyed but must be conserved as energy. Therefore, although a given physical manifestation may disintegrate, the energy itself cannot be destroyed, but returns in a different manifestation in accordance with circumstances.

KEISAKU: A flat wooden stick, about two feet long, used during zazen periods to encourage students and to remove tension from the shoulders and back. Symbolic of Manjusri Bodhisattva's Sword of Wisdom (Manjusri is the bodhisattva representing wisdom), it is usually employed only upon request.

KENSHO: Also called satori, kensho is considered essential to Rinzai Zen practice. Literally *ken* means "seeing into" and *sho* means "one's own nature." This occurs when one has broken through all one's preconceptions and has wiped away the dust covering the Mind Mirror. There are two contributing causes of kensho: accumulated samadhi and what is known as karma relation—something that triggers the experience. Although "realization" and "enlightenment" are often used as equivalent terms, it is *through* realization that one becomes enlightened.

KESSEI: An uninterrupted training period in a Zen Buddhist monastery, usually lasting one hundred days.

KINHIN: Walking zazen done between periods of sitting zazen. Kinhin is the bridge between motionless zazen and zazen in action (daily-life activities).

KOAN: An abbreviation of *kofu no andoku* (the "ko" and "an" having been put together to form one word). *Kofu* means "public" and *andoku* means "document," hence the implication of something reliable because nonsubjective. A koan is a Zen dialogue found in one of several Zen texts. It is said that about 1,700 such koans exist. However, in a broader sense, everyday life itself is a koan (the genjo koan of Soto Zen tradition). In the Rinzai Zen school, koans are used as a method of concentration during zazen; through intense unification with his koan, the student polishes his understanding.

LOTUS POSITION: A cross-legged meditation position, ideal for zazen. In the full lotus position both feet rest upon both thighs; in the half lotus position one foot rests upon the opposite thigh, usually the right foot on the left thigh.

MAHAYANA BUDDHISM: Literally, the "Great Vehicle." Its essence is a progressive and liberal spirit, which seeks, without contradicting the original teachings of the Buddha, to broaden their scope and usefulness. According to the Mahayana teaching, all beings are primarily Buddhas and can realize this in their own lifetime.

MANDALA: A consecrated geometrical representation of the universe. The symbolism found within the mandala is designed to provide unification with the forces of the universe. The use of such symbolism is primarily associated with Tibetan and Shingon (Japanese Esoteric) Buddhism.

MOKUGYO: Also called "gyorin," it is a wooden drum usually carved in the shape of a fish; used in the zendo to maintain rhythm during sutra chanting.

MU: Although the literal meaning is that of a negative syllable ("no" or "nothing"), Mu is usually used in a more positive sense as, for example, in the famous koan known as Joshu's Mu. Mu is none other than our own Mind, the formless form of the Dharma.

NEN: This important term is usually translated as "thought." However, the original Chinese character is a combination of one element meaning "present" and another meaning "mind." Therefore, a better definition would be "present-mindedness" or "mindfulness." Another meaning is "intense, single-minded thought," which, unlike prayer, has no object external to itself. Nonetheless, such thought can and does have practical consequences.

NIRVANA: Literally "extinction," both in the active and passive sense. When the fires of delusion have been blown out, the fact of original enlightenment reveals itself. Nirvana is not an abstract concept, nor some distant heaven; although often understood in a negative way as synonymous with quiescence, it has a positive, dynamic meaning and can be experienced in one's own lifetime. Nirvana is not to be confused with Parinirvana (the Buddha Shakyamuni's death). According to the Mahayana view, Nirvana is a condition analogous to the deepest samadhi, and is seen as having four essential qualities, expressed in the Japanese as *jo raku ga jo*, meaning "eternal, joyous, selfless and pure."

PRAJNA: Perhaps the single most important idea in Zen Buddhism, prajna (*hannya, J.*) is the core of the Prajnaparamita literature. It means "wisdom" or "intuitive insight." Its relationship to dhyana (meditation) is crucial. Zen practice is based on the inseparability of the two, which is revealed in zazen samadhi. Even since Hui Neng, this inseparability has been strongly emphasized.

RAKUSU: A square, patched cloth with attached straps that are hung around the neck. The rakusu itself rests on the chest. It is worn by Mahayana Buddhist monks, nuns, priests and lay devotees to symbolize the original patched robes of Shakyamuni Buddha and his disciples.

ROHATSU: Literally, "the eighth of December," an especially strenuous eight-day sesshin commemorating the Buddha's enlightenment.

ROSHI: Literally "elder teacher." A roshi is a Zen master who has received inka (Dharma acknowledgment) from his master. Essential to this transmission is the master's estimation of his student's maturity and readiness. Contrary to popular belief, the completion of the traditional koan study does not automatically mean that one is a roshi. Like the pouring of water from one cup to another, this transmission of Dharma from mind to mind is uniquely Zen in character. It usually takes at least twenty years of Zen training before the title of roshi is conferred in the Rinzai tradition. There are rare and exceptional cases of people who are truly roshis even though they have no such title. One of the ways in which the Rinzai and Soto schools differ is in the bestowing of inka.

SAMADHI: In Japanese, samadhi is translated as *shoju*, which means "right receiving." (The transliteration in Japanese is *zammai*.) Only when one has entered into samadhi can one receive things as they are; for in such a condition the mind is clear and lucid, free from impurities and impediments.

SANGHA: One of the Three Treasures of Buddhism, along with Buddha and Dharma. The original meaning is the historical assembly or brotherhood of monks and nuns surrounding Buddha Shakyamuni, but it is usually used in a broader sense to refer to any group of students of Buddhism united by their common practice. Sangha, like the other two Treasures, can be viewed from three distinct but related vantage points: the historical, the practical and the philosophical.

SEIZA: Japanese style of sitting; kneeling position.

SESSHIN: Literally "to collect the mind." Sesshin is the Buddhist seclusion or retreat, consisting of seven days of intensive zazen practice, with teisho by the roshi and dokusan a few times a day. During sesshin, the student concentrates on nothing but collecting the scattered mind so that he can realize his original unity with the universe from which he ordinarily feels separated. In Japanese monasteries, sesshins are held six or seven times a year.

SHASTRA: Literally a discourse or commentary on a sutra. One of the three divisions of the Buddhist Canon (Tripitaka). The other two are Sutra (Scriptures) and Vinaya (Precepts).

SHIKANTAZA: Literally means "nothing but (just) sitting." This is zazen in which one neither seeks enlightenment nor rejects delusion. The purest zazen, it uses no devices as such; strictly speaking, there is no goal or method. Shikantaza practice is a manifestation of original enlightenment and is, at the same time, a way toward its realization. However, the danger is that the student may overemphasize the fact of original enlightenment and underemphasize the necessity of experiencing it, with a consequent loss of intensity.

Zazen is both something one *does* and something one essentially *is*. To emphasize one aspect at the expense of the other is to misunderstand this subtle and profound practice.

SUNYATA: "Voidness" or "emptiness." Along with the Bodhisattva Vow, the doctrine of Sunyata is one of the great contributions of Mahayana Buddhism. It originated in the Madhyamika School of Nagarjuna and is the underlying theme of the Prajnaparamita literature (the *Diamond Sutra* and the *Heart Sutra* particularly). Basically, emptiness and formlessness may be identified; but this formlessness is in form and not incompatible with it. As we read in the *Heart Sutra*: "Form is emptiness, and emptiness is form." Things are empty in that they have no fixed essence, and so are nothing but the causal conditions in accordance with which they appear, disappear and reappear.

SUTRA: Literally means "scripture." The term refers either to an individual scripture or to the section of the Tripitaka containing the dialogues and discourses attributed to the historical Buddha. The other two sections are the Shastra and the Vinaya. Although attributed to the historical Buddha Shakyamuni (especially by the Theravadins), many sutras were not, in fact, delivered by him but were written considerably later. In general, the Mahayana tradition does not view sutras from a literal or fundamentalist point of view.

TATHAGATA: One of the ten epithets of the Buddha, used not only by his followers but also applied by him to himself, which gives it a special significance. There is some controversy as to the exact derivation of the term. Some claim it derives from *tatha-agata* ("thus come"), while others argue that it comes from *tatha-gata* ("thus gone"). Because the idea of the Buddha coming and/or going is inimical to the absolutist spirit of Zen, instead of interpreting this expression in this manner, Zen tends rather to locate Buddha where there is neither coming nor going—in the region of true suchness. In the words of Hakuin Zenji in *The Song of Zazen*: "Whether going or returning, we cannot be any place else." In the Mahayana-Zen tradition, Tathagata is identified with Tathata (Suchness).

TEISHO: Literally, *tei* means "to carry" and *sho* means "to declare." In a teisho the roshi tries in an immitate, concrete and vivid way to show Buddha-Dharma without resorting to any of the myriad devices and crutches of conceptualization. Normally this special form of Zen presentation takes place during sesshin and uses traditional Zen texts such as *The Gateless Gate*, *The Blue Rock Collection* or *The Sayings of Master Rinzai*.

TENZO: The cook-monk in a Zen monastery. Normally a senior student is given this job to polish his practice and to help accumulate virtue.

THERAVADA BUDDHISM: Literally, "doctrine of the Elders." One of the two mainstreams of Buddhism; considered to be the orthodox form because its scriptures are in the original Pali language. The Theravadin tradition is maintained in the countries of Sri Lanka, Burma, Thailand, Laos and Cambodia. (Mahayana Buddhism is found in China, Japan, Korea, Vietnam and the various nations of the Himalayan Mountain region.) Theravada Buddhism is also sometimes called Hinayana Buddhism.

UNSUI: Literally, "cloud and water," it is the name given to a monk still in training in a Zen monastery.

WAKA: A thirty-one-syllable Japanese poem.

ZAZEN: Literally, "sitting Zen." Although it can be interpreted in a broader sense, strictly speaking, zazen is the practice in which, sitting cross-legged on a cushion, one regulates one's breathing, disciplines one's mind and enters into an experience of one's original unity with all things. Sometimes referred to as "Zen meditation," zazen should not be considered meditation, at least not in the sense the term is generally used. The heart of the practice of Zen Buddhism, zazen is both a means to the attainment of enlightenment as well as a manifestation of original enlightenment: both something one does and something one is. Zazen practice is based on the inseparability of dhyana and prajna and is devoted to the single-minded integration of Bodhisattva spirit in one's everyday life.

ZEN: The Japanese transliteration of the Sanskrit *dhyana* (by way of a transliteration of the Chinese Ch'an). However, Zen does not mean the same as dhyana. The essence of Zen is the unity of dhyana and prajna; in practice this union is none other than zazen samadhi. The Indian practice of dhyana has a more metaphysical nature, while what is known nowadays as Zen has a much more practical, feet-on-the-ground character. Although generally considered one school of Buddhism among many, in a broader sense Zen is the heart of Buddhism as well as another name for all religions, all culture and for Mind itself. The heart of all things is the Mind that Buddha Shakyamuni realized and transmitted to his successor and that has been transmitted in the Zen tradition century after century.

ZENDO: The place where formal zazen is practiced.

ZENJI: *Ji* is written with two different characters. The first means "teacher." In this sense *Zenji* means "Zen teacher" or "Zen master." The second means "fellow" or "person." Here Zenji is roughly the same as *unsui*—that is, "a monk practicing in a monastery." In America, however, the term is most often used in contrast to *Koji* ("layman") and in referring to a Zen master in the past (*e.g.*, Hakuin Ekaku Zenji).